New England Quaker Meetinghouses

Past and Present

By Silas B. Weeks

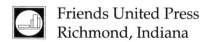 Friends United Press
Richmond, Indiana

Printed in the United States of America

Book design by Shari Pickett Veach
Cover design by Julia Jensen

Front Cover: Dover (NH) Friends Meetinghouse photo by Charlotte Fardelmann.
Back Cover: Uxbridge (MA) Friends Meetinghouse photo by Silas B. Weeks.

We are grateful to the Obadiah Brown Benevolent Fund
for a grant toward the publication of this book.

Library of Congress Cataloging-in-Publication Data

Weeks, Silas B. (Silas Burling), 1914-   Maine Author
    New England Quaker Meetinghouses: past and present / by Silas B. Weeks.
        p. cm.
    Includes bibliographical references and index.
    ISBN 0-944350-51-8 ✓
        1. Quaker church buildings—New England. 2. Quakers—New England—History. I.
    Title.

NA5215 .W44 2001
289.6'74—dc21   2001023709

Contents

Foreword:
Quiet Grace

The Friends Meetinghouse as an expression of faith gives testimony to leadings of simplicity and modesty, humility and equality. Purposely made without a caring for fashion, meetinghouses decidedly were fashioned with a caring that results in an unadorned elegance and grace. This raiment of simplicity imbues these meetinghouses with quiet resplendence. The spirit that is felt to inhabit them is expressed in the clear and simple lines of the architecture and in the light-filled interiors.

The temple of the Living God is but the human body. And Quakers felt that direct experience of the Inner Light was of utmost importance. But, this experience is enhanced when meeting together. "Where two or more are gathered." And the gathered meeting empowered the assembled to go inside to greet the Light, to go inside to gain outlook. The clear relation of that within to that without bespeaks the concern that the life lived reflects the Inner Ideal.

As soul is embodied, so is the body housed. While housing the body of the meeting was central to the Quaker community, that the structure not be overly self-important seems evident. The congruence of inside to outside of self is also evident in the relation between the calm sensibility of the interior to the stately quietude of the exterior of the meetinghouse. As you examine these New England Quaker Meetinghouses you will find writ in this humble architecture the presence of a plain people seeking direct contact with a simple Truth.

James A. Turrell

Preface:
Quaker Theology and Meetinghouse Design

Factual information about Quaker meetinghouses and their histories may well be interesting to the general reader and especially of interest to Friends. Unless there is some understanding of why meetinghouses look the way they do, however, the essence that gives them their "Quaker character" will never be appreciated.

The theology of religious sects is reflected to varying degrees in the architecture of their places of worship. Temples, mosques, cathedrals, churches, and meetinghouses are all recognizably different in design. Each expresses in architectural terms something of the beliefs held by the religion.

These Quaker meetinghouses, in their very simplicity, often stand out as architecturally unique in the communities in which they were built. Indeed, it would be hard to imagine a stronger visual statement about the Quaker values of simplicity and economy than in the elegant austerity of their eighteenth-century houses, or about the vitality of early Quakerism in New England than in, for example, the Great Meetinghouse at Newport, Rhode Island.

Quaker testimonies of simplicity, equality, and community are often reflected in meetinghouse design, although the houses themselves were simply viewed as providing a convenient place to meet and were not regarded as more or less holy than other places. Early Friends, in fact, often kept their hats on during meeting for worship for this reason. The earlier buildings were unadorned. They had no towers, bells, crosses, or stained glass; their interiors had no altars or organs. The earliest structures in America were built in the basic colonial foursquare Georgian or Federal style, of post and beam construction. Others were of cape design, without overhang at the eaves or gable ends. In the 1800s the Greek Revival style became common.

The two entry doors—one for women and one for men—symbolized the equality between the sexes. Although women and men sat on separate sides of the house and had separate meetings for business, women rose to preach during meeting for worship as often as men. During meetings for business, a wooden partition separated the men and women so they would be able to discuss their particular concerns separately and alone. Although this may today appear as inequality, it must be remembered that in the seventeenth and eighteenth centuries it was unheard of for women to preach or to conduct business on an equal footing with men. The partitions evinced a respect for privacy more than a wish to segregate men and women.

The tenet of simplicity is often reflected inside the meetinghouses as well as in their austere exteriors. Inside, plain wooden benches were set in the center of the room, with one or two raised facing benches at the front. These benches traditionally accommodated the elders and "ministers," who were members of recognized spiritual maturity, called "weighty Friends." There was no ornamentation of any kind, and the walls were usually painted "Quaker gray."

In 1827-28 Friends in Philadelphia, New York, and Ohio Yearly meetings split into two groups: Orthodox and Hicksite. The "Great Separation" was centered on the place of the Bible in the Quaker belief system. Later, in the 1840s and 50s, there was a further split among Orthodox Friends in England (1845) and Ohio (1854) between the followers of Joseph John Gurney and John Wilbur. Along with Gurneyite Orthodoxy came acceptance of pastors and music in some Friends meetings. The Friends became known as pastoral Friends, and they began building structures that were a departure from traditional buildings and became known as Friends churches. Sometimes these churches might have a modest tower, but never a steeple. The country structures remained fairly typical of earlier ones, except that that double doors and divided interior doors were eliminated, as were the facing benches, which were replaced with a formal lectern. The seats tended to be more like pews than the old-fashioned benches. Urban Friends churches were similar to Protestant churches except that they rarely had towers or steeples, stained glass windows, or bells. They were sometimes built of brick. Inside, dividers were dispensed with, and a simple lectern replaced the facing benches. In New England today only a few of these structures remain in use by pastoral Friends.

Until recent times, nonpastoral meetinghouses tended to retain their traditional features, including double entry doors, a divided interior with movable shutters, and a raised facing bench. A substantial number of the earlier buildings were of two stories, with an interior gallery and, frequently, an entrance vestibule. The buildings were almost always of frame construction (usually post and beam) and were plain to the point of severity both outside and inside.

In contrast, more recently built nonpastoral meetinghouses have tended to be largely single story, and double doors and divided interiors are no longer used. Seating arrangements have also changed; the benches usually face each other in a hollow square, without the traditional facing benches at the front. Interiors and exteriors remain plain, but they are of a more finished nature. Interiors now also include items never present in older buildings, such as bathrooms, kitchens, library space, and First Day schoolrooms

Some Friends may remark, "Never mind those old meetinghouses—the Society of Friends is a religious community, not a set of buildings." I dare say that those same Friends would be shocked if it were suggested that the journals of George Fox, John Woolman, Elias Hicks, and other archival records be thrown away. I maintain that the meetinghouses—old and new, pastoral and nonpastoral—as well as the burial grounds and other structures—are as important a part of Quaker heritage as any written documents. Structures are merely another kind of record.

The matter of acknowledgments in a project like this is extremely difficult because so many people have helped in so many ways.

With each meetinghouse I have tried to indicate my source of information, especially if a person provided it. I am indebted to the archivists at New England Quaker Archives in Providence, Rhode Island—in particular to Rosalind Wiggins. Elizabeth Moger of the New York Yearly Meeting Haviland Records office was similarly helpful. The staff in charge of Quaker records at both the historical society in Portland, Maine, and at Swarthmore and Haverford colleges also provided invaluable assistance.

Anne Humes, Ralph Greene, Thyra Jane Foster, Shirley Leslie, and Elwyn

Meader sent me extensive information about a number of meetinghouses that would otherwise have not been available. My life-long friend and former college roommate, Franklin Denning, saved me miles of travel by taking excellent photos of meeting-houses on the Cape; his wife Jeannette followed up with relevant clippings from area papers. Friend Bruce French went out of his way to get special photos of the new meetinghouse in New Haven, Connecticut.

My son, Charter Weeks, and his wife, Marie Harris, encouraged me to "get at it" and gave me the benefit of their professional advice. Friend Jean Davis unscrambled my badly typed original manuscript and put everything in the computer, making Elizabeth Knies' detailed editing a simpler chore. Elizabeth's sharp eye and relevant questions considerably improved the final product. My wife, Constance, put up with many unplanned diversions on journeys made for other purposes. She has been a great support in a project that has now lasted years, instead of the months that I first envisioned.

As this project entered its final editing Kathleen Flanagan's sharp eye identified added questions about certain facts and need for clarity, which were most helpful. In dealing with some of those questions I had further help from archivists at the New England Yearly Meeting Archives and Historical Records and Rhode Island Historical Society, including Richard Stattler and Amy Lappin.

Lastly I am much indebted to the Obadiah Brown Benevolent Fund for financial support and to Barbara Bennett Mays, Friends United Press, for her continued over-sight and support.

Introduction

Over fifteen years ago, for reasons not entirely clear to me, I decided to photograph all the Quaker meetinghouses in New England. I was vaguely familiar with a number of the more active meetings. The then newly released map of New England meetings led me to think it would not be a particularly daunting job. I thought it would be interesting to see if distinct differences in building styles existed among the houses of unprogrammed and pastoral meetings. My interest was sparked by the fact that I have always had a strong visual affinity for the clear and simple lines of early New England buildings, whether houses, barns, sheds, churches, or meetinghouses.

The project turned out to be larger than anticipated. Although New England's six states could collectively be tucked into the state of Texas, the high density of towns and cities often made finding a particular meetinghouse like looking for the needle in the haystack. For example, Smithfield Meeting is in Woonsocket, and Unity Meeting is just "out there some place."

Getting from here to there and back again consumed substantially more time, energy, and money than I had originally envisioned. Much of the fieldwork was done as a by-product of other trips, on which my wife frequently accompanied me, suffering (not always in silence) over delays and detours. Locating a particular meetinghouse often became an excuse for an excursion that we might not otherwise have taken.

The task was enlarged by what is perhaps best described as "creeping complexity." It became immediately apparent that a photograph by itself was not enough. In order to find out something about the history of a given structure, I developed a form that I sent to meeting clerks with a request for descriptive materials. The forms were returned in various states: fairly complete, fairly incomplete—or sometimes not at all. They included statements such as "this is the third meetinghouse here since 1804."

And so the project grew. What about those two other meetinghouses? Where and when did they exist? Did either still stand? If so, what was their present use? Could a photo be obtained? What about the site itself—was it marked, as in the case of Grande Isle Vermont, or unmarked, as in the case of New Durham, New Hampshire? What about the burial ground?

The first trip was to the New England Yearly Meeting archives in Providence, Rhode Island, to check photographs already on hand and to ask for advice. There, Rosalind Wiggins and the archive committee gladly extended help and support. Later journeys included a visit to the photo section of the Library of Congress in the new Madison Building, the Quaker Archives at Swarthmore College, and a visit to the Maine Historical Society in Portland, Maine. There was some useful correspondence with the Vermont Historical Society as well.

The Chart of Vital Statistics of New England Friends Meetings prepared by Thyra Jane Foster details the evolution of various present and past Quaker meetings. This information provided the basis for choosing what to follow up. In the case of meetings that are no longer active, I have depended on correspondence with knowledgeable Friends, and especially on local town libraries, which were often able to provide copies of materials dealing with past church organizations that had been published in town histories.

Friend Louis Marstaller supplied me with a set of glass-covered slides of many meetinghouse pictures taken during the 1930s by James A. Coney, a Friends pastor at North Berwick, Maine, which included a number of meetinghouses now torn down.

Regarding the narrative statements about the various buildings and sites, I can only say that they represent the best (or the only) information I was able to acquire. This does not mean that there isn't a great deal more information to be unearthed. In some cases, what is recorded is either my personal understanding or a condensation of materials sent me, and I accept the responsibility for whatever mistakes may be present.

Some of the material from historical reports is either suspect or in error. For example, two different sources may disagree about the same material, or a single source may contain an obvious error, as in the case of a site marker in my home town of Eliot, Maine, where a plaque proclaims the "Site of First Quaker Meetinghouse in Maine, 1768." This was not the first meetinghouse site in Maine; rather, it was the site (the building is long gone) of a former Dover, New Hampshire, meetinghouse that had been moved there.

I have chosen to organize the project by states, since this makes more sense than doing it by "quarters." [Ed. Note: Quarters are geographical divisions with Quaker church polity.] Within each state, material is organized by meetinghouses currently standing (whether they are in use by Quakers or not), meetinghouses no longer standing, and cemeteries.

I hope that knowledgeable readers who review these materials will write to me and point out any mistakes I may have made. I will hand their comments on to the next person to continue this study.

Finally, since this book is about Quaker meetinghouses, it only includes information on Quaker meetings that own their worship space. (The one exception is Beacon Hill Friends Meeting that meets in historic Beacon Hill Friends House.) A list of all Friends meetings in New England is available from the New England Yearly Meeting office, 901 Pleasant Street, Worcester MA 01602.

Connecticut

Connecticut

Locating meetinghouses in Connecticut was somewhat difficult, in part because they were far enough away from my home in Maine to require specially planned trips, and in part because some past and present-day meetings in Connecticut belong to New York Yearly Meeting, while others belong to New England Yearly Meeting.

It was no problem to find the new structures at Storrs and New London. New London was unusual, in that the meetinghouse there was formerly a church. While many meetinghouses have been converted for use by churches, I don't know of another case of a church becoming a meetinghouse.

I had known about and visited the meetinghouse at Hartford, a relatively new structure made of brick. If the burying ground at this meeting looks a bit un-Quakerly, it is probably because it was previously a cemetery for another church. This meeting was originally under the care of New York Yearly Meeting; it was laid down during the Civil War and restarted in 1938 under the care of New England Yearly Meeting.

Wilton Meeting supplied me with a copy of their historical statement, which was of great help, as was the extensive material on Stamford-Greenwich sent by clerk Nancy Nothhelfer. The Stamford meetinghouse is another example of a converted building; it had been Stamford's last one-room school, which had closed in 1948. This school building was on a site formerly used by a Baptist church. The first meeting held in that community was in 1699; it was re-established in 1811 by Catharine Selleck sitting alone in silence. A meetinghouse was built, but it lasted only a few years and I do not have information on its site. Charles Swan of East Hartford and Old Orchard Beach, Maine, who has often visited my home, is a wonderful source of information about past Quaker buildings. He feels sure there was one in Quaker Farms that was converted to another use. I expect to make a personal visit there to see if I can find it.

Looking at an early map in the Swarthmore College archives that showed the location of New England meetinghouses, I noted that there had been one in Pomfret. When I visited the town, I was fortunate enough to find materials in the local library, including a fine pen and ink sketch of the meetinghouse, which itself is now long gone.

Connecticut Meetinghouses

Hartford Friends Meetinghouse

Hartford, Connecticut
Erected: 1950
Location: Quaker Lane
Burial Ground: Yes
In Use as Quaker Meetinghouse

In 1780 a group of Quaker families from Duchess County, New York, settled in West Hartford and formed a meeting. In 1799 they acquired land for and built a meetinghouse. There was also a school and a cemetery. The meeting declined as members began moving to Ohio around 1830. In 1842, the meetinghouse was sold to St. James Episcopal Church and the school was leased to the East Side School District. In 1852, the two buildings were combined and moved from the east side of Quaker Lane to the west side. An historical plaque at the site states that the building was destroyed by fire. The town maintained a small, fenced portion of the cemetery. There is speculation about whether John Greenleaf Whittier attended this meeting while living in Hartford, but the claim has not been authenticated.

The present meeting on Quaker Lane was started in 1937. Under the care of New England Yearly Meeting it became a Monthly Meeting in 1940. Hartford Monthly Meeting applied to New York Yearly Meeting for a quit-claim deed for the land on Quaker Lane. The single-story brick building in use now on that land was erected in 1950. Alexander Purdy delivered the dedication address. A brick addition was made to the building in 1960.

Several large monuments, originally in front of the building, marked the graves of Friends buried there in the late nineteenth century.

SOURCES: Tom Bodine, Barbara Taylor, and V. Martin (Hartford Public Library).

Miriam Swartz

Housatonic Friends Meetinghouse

Bruce French

New Haven Friends Meetinghouse

Housatonic (New Milford), Connecticut
Erected: 1805
Location: Route 7, south of New Milford
Burial Ground: Yes
In Use as Quaker Meetinghouse

This meetinghouse, the second in the Housatonic area, was raised in 1805 on land deeded in 1788. It continued in use until later in the 1800s. A local worship group became a preparative meeting in the 1950s, and in 1969 acquired the vacant building, which was stripped of benches. They undertook its restoration and opened for worship on 5th month 7th, 1970. In 1972 an arsonist set fire to the house, but it was not destroyed; repairs were made the following year. This meeting had a long history of association with the Oblong Meeting at Pawling, New York.

There is a burial ground on the site of the original meetinghouse, north of the present meetinghouse, and a second one at the present site. Both are under the care of the New Milford Cemetery Association.

SOURCE: 1993 Directory, New York Yearly Meeting, supplied by Miriam O. Swartz of Danbury, Connecticut.

New Haven, Connecticut
Erected: 1995
Location: 225 East Grand Avenue
Burial Ground: No
In Use as Quaker Meetinghouse

During the 1980s, Friends in New Haven used a meeting room on the Yale University campus. Eventually a search was initiated to find a new space that would be their own. In 1990 a property was acquired, but difficulties with its conversion and expansion made it unsatisfactory.

Then a two-acre plot on East Grand Avenue, which had previously been considered, became available for $120,000, a price much lower than its original one, architect Charlotte Hitchcock worked closely with Friends to create a contemporary style, two-story building with 2,400 square feet of space on each floor. Financing for the $480,000 building contract came from the sale of the previous property, fundraising activities, and a loan from the Friends General Conference Meetinghouse Fund.

The meetinghouse has a thirty-six foot square meeting room on the second floor, with oak flooring, a beamed ceiling, a fireplace, and continuous windows along the south and west sides. A library and bathrooms are also on the second floor, while an assembly room, classrooms, and a kitchen occupy the lower floor. The building was first occupied in June of 1995.

SOURCE: William Graustein, New Haven, Connecticut.

pleted the exterior painting at a cost of $3,000 dollars, using funds raised by members and a local grant. They have also shored up the original building twice, recently putting in a new foundation and pulling in the walls. There is still no plumbing and no running water, but there is heat, a gas-fired toilet, and they carry in jugs of water. The addition of running water and a bathroom awaits additional funds.

SOURCE: Joan Warren, clerk of building committee.

New London Friends Meetinghouse

Stamford-Greenwich Friends Meetinghouse

Waterford, Connecticut
Erected: 1918
Location: 176 Oswegatchie Road, Waterford
Burial ground: No
In Use as Quaker Meetinghouse

In 1985, Friends in New London acquired an old Episcopalian summer chapel and are in the process of rehabilitating it. (There is no steeple, says Joan Warren; the steeple fell and the meeting chose not to replace it.) The meeting has com-

Stamford-Greenwich, Connecticut
Erected: circa 1840
Location: 572 Roxbury Road, Stamford
Burial Ground: No
In Use as Quaker Meetinghouse

Thomas Story was among the Quakers who first appeared in Stamford in 1699, but they were forced to leave shortly thereafter by the town constable because Quakerism was against the laws of the state. Then meeting was established in 1811 and a meetinghouse built, but again the meeting was short-lived.

The present meeting started as an informal worship group in June of 1948; in 1949 it became a preparative meeting under the care of Purchase (New York) Monthly Meeting.

In 1951, the old Bangall Schoolhouse on the corner of Westover and Roxbury Roads (the last one room school in Stamford) was purchased together with the land then owned and leased to the city by the Stamford Baptist Church. Benches for the meetinghouse came from the old Purchase Meetinghouse and from the Scarsdale Meeting. The benches from Scarsdale had originally been in the 15th Street Meeting in New York City.

In November 1953, the meeting formally became the Stamford-Greenwich Monthly Meeting in the Purchase Quarter. In that same year, plans were made to add a new meeting room and a shell (erected in 1954). In 1956 work was started on a connecting wing between the old school house and the new meeting room; it was completed in 1958. The new wing included plumbing and heating, as well as kitchen and bathroom facilities. The new addition was designed by Lawrence Greene of New Canaan. Funds for the improvements were raised by friends and members and by a loan from New York Monthly Meeting.

SOURCES: Jack DeForest and Nancy Nothhelfer.

Storrs Friends Meetinghouse

Storrs, Connecticut
Erected: 1950s
Location: 57 Hunting Lodge Road
Burial Ground: No
In Use as Quaker Meetinghouse

The original structure was a two-story cinderblock and brick building originally built and used as cooperative nursery school. It was acquired for meeting use in the 1970s and had a main meeting room on the second floor that opened at ground level on one side, as the building is built into an embankment. First Day rooms are on the lower-level floor. The building was built by Joseph Kovarouics.

A major addition in 1997 added a foyer and a new meeting room with windows on three sides. The architect, John Talgo, paid special attention to acoustics for the new worship space. The new addition has a wood exterior and changed the entire orientation of the building.

SOURCES: Lawrence Parish, Stuart Kermes, and Norman Janes.

Wilton Friends Meetinghouse

Wilton, Connecticut
Erected: 1952
Location: 317 New Canaan Road
Burial Ground: No
In Use as Quaker Meetinghouse

Friends in the Wilton area first gathered at the home of Henry Fraad in Weston in 1938 and later in various other places, including Norwalk, West Port, and New Canaan. In July of 1942, the group became a regular preparative meeting under the care of Purchase (New York) Monthly Meeting. In 1947, this became Fairfield County Monthly Meeting. Later, with the rise of other Friends groups in the county, the name was changed in 1957 to Wilton Monthly Meeting.

In 1947, Gayer and Eleanor Dominick made a gift of five acres of land in Wilton, on which the first section of the present meetinghouse (at 317 New Canaan Road) was completed in December of 1952. Another section, including the present meeting room, was added in 1954, and an exten-sion for the First Day school was completed in 1964/65.

A nursery school under the care of the meeting has been in operation since 1956. The school is named after Helen Gander, a Friend instrumental in founding the meeting. A separate building on meeting property houses the Connecticut Friends School for grades K-6, which opened in the fall of 1999. Wilton Friends Meeting is affiliated with New York Yearly Meeting.

SOURCE: Marjorie Walton, clerk of Wilton Monthly Meeting, February 1986 and October 2000.

Connecticut Meetinghouses No Longer Standing

Canaan, Connecticut

There was a meetinghouse in Canaan located near the corner of Canaan Valley Road and Moses Mead Road. I have not been able to find data regarding its size or exact date of construction. The meeting itself was established (that is, "allowed") in 1807; it became a preparative meeting in 1820 under the care of Nine Partners Meeting of New York Yearly Meeting, so it seems likely that there was a house by that time. The orthodox Friends use of the building was laid down in 1828, but the Hicksite Friends continued using it until 1838.

The building was taken down in 1876. Part of the frame was used in David Donald's new horse barn, which was raised on the afternoon of June 9, 1876, with thirty men helping. Still later a schoolhouse occupied the site; it eventually became a small dwelling. A burying ground adjoins the site, next to the Carlson family plot. The Carlson family maintains both. The only headstones bear dates after 1850, although we may assume that there were many earlier burials that went unmarked, in keeping with early Quaker practice.

Pomfret, Connecticut

Pomfret history records that there was a Friends meetinghouse built in 1805 on land given by Obed Dennis near Roland Baker's home, about an eighth of a mile west of discontinued Quaker Road at the foot of Pomfret Hill. A Mr. Porter is recorded as the first minister.

Promfret Friends Meetinghouse (NLS)

The house was encircled by a wall or fence and had a closed gate. It was a two-story structure measuring twenty by forty feet. It faced south and had chimneys on either end. There were separate entrance doors for men and women and partitions that divided the men's section from the women's for business meetings. A gallery wrapped around the second story. There was a small burying ground at the rear and a larger one located a half-mile west on the main street.

There were apparently only a few Friends living in Pomfret at the time, but others came from Brooklyn, Killingly, and Abington. One report has it that the building burned about 1900, after years of disuse, while another puts the date about 1920.

SOURCE: *Folklore and Firesides of Pomfret, Hampton, and Vicinity* by Susan Jewett Griggs, Chapter 7, pages 81-82.

Quaker Burial Grounds in Connecticut

Canaan, Connecticut—

At site of original meetinghouse, near corner of Canaan Valley road and Moses Mead Road.

Hartford, Connecticut—

On Quaker Lane in front of meetinghouse.

Housatonic, Connecticut—

1.) At site of original meetinghouse, north of present meetinghouse;

2.) adjacent to present meetinghouse on Route 7 north of Lanesville Road and south of New Milford. Both cemeteries under the care of the New Milford Cemetery Association.

Pomfret, Connecticut—

1.) At site of original meetinghouse, an eighth of a mile west of end of Quaker Road, at foot of Pomfret Hill;

2.) Half a mile west of original meetinghouse, on main street.

Maine

Maine

The first Friends meeting in Maine was held by three women in South Berwick in 1666—probably the same women Sheriff Waldron later drove out of the area tied to the back of an ox cart. The first regular meeting was held in Kittery (possibly in the area now called Eliot) in 1740, and the second in Falmouth about 1746. At the start of World War I, there were twenty-three active meetings in Maine with a total membership of 1800. In 1991, counting worship groups, there were twenty-four meetings.

Maine has a great variety of structures, including an interesting set of Friends churches and two of the newer meetinghouses in New England, at Cobscook in Whiting and at Damariscotta. The site for the Cobscook meetinghouse on Lubec Road was a gift. Lumber for building the structure was cut from members' farms, and labor was donated by skilled carpenter members. Work days and special materials were also contributed, as were benches from a New York meetinghouse. The finished structure measures twenty-six by forty feet and is estimated to have cost about $15,000, not counting labor, land, or donated materials.

Information about Quakers in Appleton, written up by Marie K. Hammond, was furnished me by her daughter, Cynthia Geady, of Cape Elizabeth. There are fifteen pages gleaned from a painstaking search of records at the Maine Historical Society, which performs certain archival work for New England Yearly Meeting. Much of the Appleton material deals with disownment of members, including Stephen Gushee who reported his son for having joined the Free Masons and for marrying out of the meeting; Silas and Joseph Burton for having departed from plainness in dress and address and for performing military duty; and T.-J. for employing P.-D. to keep his house and for committing the crime of fornication with her. The case of Peleg Lincoln, "who has removed into the limits of St. Albans Monthly Meeting without paying his just debts and left his affairs in a manner injurious to the credit of the Society," is also reported. Peleg later made amends and was reinstated. Charles Dinsmore was labored with for departure from Friends in dress and address and attending dancing school. The document contains many other names and details of meetings in nearby Hope, China, and other towns.

Assistance in finding information about buildings in the state has come to me from a great variety of sources and persons. For example, my insurance agent, Paul Sinnott, who lives in Lewiston, was kind enough to take a photo of the former Friends church there and send it to me.

Sidney Meeting records contain, as do many others, some wonderful Friends first names, including Content, Harper, Zadock, Eliphalic, and Peace. One entry notes: "Hannah Weeks (no relative of mine!) is addicted to the custom of too freely partaking of spirituous liquors. She has been labored with to no avail."

A complete history of the South China meeting (now the South China Community Church) was compiled by Miriam Jones Brown and Evelyn Jones Wicke. It includes materials about Dirigo, China, South China, and Pond meetings, as well as about Vassalboro and Oak Grove. In addition, it gives names and family information about important Quaker leaders of the past, notably about Rufus Jones, who grew up in the area and became one of the leading lights of Quakerism in the twentieth century. The Pond Meetinghouse, which Rufus attended on occasion, is now located at Friends China Camp. He wrote: "The history of Friends in this country can never be adequately written since from their first appearance until the present time, they have done their work in quiet, unobtrusive ways leaving behind little more record...than nature does in her unobserved workings in the forest." The Quaker population in the area has declined greatly over the years.

A town history of Unity, Maine contains extensive notes on Quakers there. It begins by saying that Quakers first established themselves in Eliot in 1730 and grew in numbers throughout the remainder of the century, establishing churches in Falmouth, South Berwick (should be North Berwick), Durham, and Windham, "much to the consternation of the Congregationalists who were alarmed at other sects appearing in Maine."

Ralph Cook of Pembroke, a member of the Cobscook meeting, wrote to alert me about the fate of some of the more recent Friends structures after he saw a note about my meetinghouse project in the *New England Friend*. He asked what I might have in the way of meetinghouse photos that might be of interest to the building committee at Cobscook, who were then considering meetinghouse design. I was able to lend them nineteen different pictures.

Durham is one of the actively flourishing meetings in the state. It is fortunate in having a quite complete written record of its history, prepared by Hattie Cox. This report, as in the case of South China, contains information about connections with other nearby meetings in the quarter, including Lewiston, Greene, Wales, Leeds, Wilton, Pownal, and Litchfield. The report says that in 1828 Waitsill Webber was employed to shingle the fore side of the meetinghouse and make what repairs were needed to the same with good materials and in a worklike manner for the sum of $28. This happens to be less then I paid for just two bundles of wood shingles in the summer of 1987. The house was burned the next year, apparently from a spark from the blacksmith shop across the way. A new building of brick, one-story high and sixty by forty feet, was erected. In 1900 a recommendation for remodeling the structure carried the proviso that a sum of $750 should first be raised so that no debt would be incurred. Major revisions were made.

Marion Hussey, a personal friend and member of the Dover, New Hampshire meeting was most helpful with facts about the history of meetinghouses of various periods in North Berwick. The Hussey family, manufacturers of the famous Hussey plow, was for many years prominent among Quakers in the area. The business is ongoing, but it no longer makes agricultural implements. Marion's husband, Phillip, took part in a play held in the Dover Meeting yard in the summer of 1964. The play was "Mother Whittier's Meeting" written by Henry Bailey Stevens, a member of Dover Meeting. Also taking part, were William Penn Tuttle and his son Hugh, of the famous Tuttle's Red Barn Farm on Dover Neck.

While visiting the village of Casco, I saw a sign on the local historical society's building—"Friends School." Upon inquiry, I was told that this former one-room public school had been located a short distance past the meetinghouse. Because so many of the students were Friends, it was always known locally as the Friends School.

The history of Kennebec County contains a wonderful item about the Friends church in Winthrop. In 1878, a general meeting was held there "at which time the spirit of the Lord was abundantly poured out. Fully three thousand attended in one day and many souls were brought from darkness to light."

Among the many people to whom I owe thanks for their generous help is Ralph Greene, a Friends pastor. My research in Maine was greatly aided by material from his master's thesis, *The Development of Quaker Communities in Central Maine—1770 to 1800.*

Maine Meetinghouses

Brooks Friends Meetinghouse

Brooks, Maine
Erected: 1822
Location: On Route 7 (Moose Head Trail)
   on way to Woods Jackson
Burial Ground: Yes
Not in Use as Quaker Meetinghouse

The meetinghouse in Brooks was built in 1822. Brooks became a monthly meeting in 1837 when it split off from China Monthly Meeting. Membership was listed at fifty at that time, but declined over the years due to "marrying out." The remaining members became associated with other religious bodies.

The meetinghouse was sold to the Harvest Home Grange No. 52 in 1919. They still occupy the building in its original form. The former horse sheds no longer stand, but the burying ground is in good shape and is under the care of the town. Quaker names of past members include Jones, Varney, Moulton, Sharpless, Winslow, and

Hussey. It is reported that the various religious groups in town worked in harmony.

Source: *Sketches of Brooks History*, by Seth W. Norwood and Rhoda Smith, secretary of Brooks Harvest Home Grange No. 52.

Quaker Ridge Meetinghouse

Casco, Maine
Erected: 1814
Location: Quaker Ridge Road
Burial Ground: Yes
In Use as Quaker Meetinghouse (summers only)
National Register of Historical Buildings

The Casco meetinghouse is the oldest standing house in Maine, but not the first. Of particular interest is its divided interior. The right side is typically simple, plain post and beam with wide boards. It has high-backed benches, wainscoting under the windows and facing bench. Hinged panels, which can be lowered for meeting for business, are hooked to the ceiling.

The left side is quite different, with a harmonium at the front, a divided aisle, and elaborate, curved pews. This side reflects the worship style among some New England Friends following the visit in 1838-40 of Joseph John Gurney, a British evangelical Quaker. This trend reached its height in the late 1800s. The mystery is, why one side and not both?

There are two dates for either restructuring or enlargement of the building—1846 and "about 1860"—and a date of 1890 for the fancy pews.

Quakers moved into Casco in 1802 from nearby Windham and built the meetinghouse in 1814 on land acquired from Daniel Cook. Two meetings were held in the building beginning in 1841 and several years following when Casco split off from Raymond. Membership declined and from 1921 to 1956 Windham Friends held meeting there once a year. After that, Friends from Philadelphia, who summered nearby, took over care of the building and established regular meeting for worship in July and August. It is reported that these continue and that the door is unlatched and anyone may enter and register their name in a guest book.

There are two associated Friends burying grounds nearby.

Sources: National Register of Historic Places, July 1975 and Elizabeth Maxfield-Miller, Cambridge Friends Meeting.

Ralph Greene

Neck Friends Meetinghouse

China, Maine
Location: Route 202 at a junction with the road to the town dump and near the Town Office building.
Burial ground: Yes. Across China Lake on Neck Road near the end of the road's dead end.
No Longer in Use as Quaker Meetinghouse

The Neck Meetinghouse (from the designation China Neck) was moved across China Lake a number of years ago to be used as a barn. Current sources are not sure if it was dragged across the ice in winter or floated across in warmer weather. The meetinghouse has been very well maintained as a barn. The nearby house was destroyed by fire in the late 1990s.

Families of Friends began to settle in China, Maine in 1774. They attended meetings in Vassalboro or Durham when able. Regular meetings for worship began in China in 1802, under Vassalboro Monthly Meeting.

New England Yearly Meeting Archives show dates for Neck worship group from 1826-1855; the name then changed to West China preparative meeting, with records from 1855-1921.

One of the slaves of an early Quaker is buried in the associated Quaker burial ground on Route 202.

Source: Ralph Greene, Orland, Maine. New England Yearly Meeting Archives.

Pond Meetinghouse, China, Maine

China, Maine (Pond Meetinghouse)
Erected: 1807
Location: Route 202 on Lakeview Drive
Not in Use as Quaker Meetinghouse; part of
Friends China Camp

This plain, single-story, thirty-foot by forty-foot white clapboard structure with extended two door vestibule has a long and interesting history. The builders were Ruben Fairfield, James Meader, Isaac Hussey, and Jedediah Jepson.

The building was used for town meetings a number of times in the early 1800s. In its earlier days it was heated with a "potash stove"—a large iron kettle turned upside down on a brick hearth, on which members warmed their soap stones.

This group was set off as Harlem Monthly Meeting in 1813. The name changed to China Monthly Meeting in 1825.

Rufus Jones reportedly attended here when Quarterly Meeting met. In 1907, five dollars was raised at a centennial celebration to "place a suitable tablet on the venerable building giving the names of the committee and date of erection," which was done.

Membership declined after this date and the house closed down in 1915. In 1930 the Zonta Club of Augusta established a summer camp on the site for children with tuberculosis. Renovations including bedrooms, a kitchen, and chemical toilets were made at that time. The camp lasted until 1937, when the principal promoter, Marion Fox Oaks, died.

The building stood idle until 1953, when the New England Yearly Meeting agreed to establish a camp for young Friends at the site. Since then, more land (including lake frontage) and buildings have been added. The old meetinghouse has been converted to a crafts center. In 9th month 1961, China Monthly Meeting sold their interest in the property to the New England Yearly Meeting for one dollar. There is an adjacent burial ground.

SOURCE: Materials furnished by Evelyn Wicke, South China, Maine, including a brief history written by Mary Grow in 1982. Also, New England Yearly Meeting Archives.

South China Friends Meetinghouse
(Now South China Community Church)

South China, Maine
Erected: 1884
Location: Main Street
Burial Ground: Yes; across the street from
the meetinghouse
Used by Quakers; owned by another
denomination

Friends in South China attended meeting in
Dirigo until the South China Church was built.
China Monthly Meeting was organized in 1813
and other meetinghouses were also built at China
Neck, Dirigo, and "the Pond" (the local nickname
for China Lake).

The South China Meetinghouse was built on
the site of a former Baptist church that had
burned in 1869; the lot was transferred to Friends
for one dollar. The building committee consisted
of Josiah Philbrook and Walter, William, Frank,
and Jeremiah Jones.

The original building was a one-and-a-half
story, single-room structure with gabled ends,
facing the street. Later, two small rooms and a
tower were added, and the front door was
relocated. At one time horse sheds stood on an
adjacent strip of land purchased for $15. Later
additions included a Sunday School room and a
pastor's study. In recent years considerable
interior and exterior upgrades have been made,
including new windows, a septic system, and a
furnace.

In 1935 the church was reorganized into a
South China Community Church. A Friends
Monthly Meeting continues to use the building.

There is an associated cemetery, Jones Cemetery, across the street. Also across the street from
the meetinghouse is South China Library, which
was started by the meeting and has a large
genealogy collection.

There are six scattered Quaker burial
grounds, three under the care of the town, and
three under the care of China Monthly Meeting.
Of these last three, one is located on Village Street,
in China, one is on Lakeview Road, and one is on
China Neck Road on the northwest side of China
Lake, looking from China.

SOURCE: *History of South China Community Church, 1884-
1984.* Additional information supplied by Evelyn Wicke and
Jean Dempster, South China.

Midcoast Friends Meetinghouse

Damariscotta, Maine (Midcoast Meeting)
Erected: 1995
Location: 2/10 mile off Route 1. From the south
turn left at blinker
In Use as Quaker Meetinghouse

This new structure was completed 5th month, 26th, 1995. The process started in 1990 when the space at the Skidompha Library that had been used for eighteen years was no longer available.

In 1992 a search committee was established. It eventually expanded to become the meetinghouse committee. It convened for the first time in the 9th month 1992. A search was started for land, and 2.7 acres were obtained from George Freeman in 2nd month 1994.

A seed-money gift of $50,000 from Jim St. John initiated fundraising efforts that eventually netted about $120,000 in gifts, pledges, and monies from fundraising projects. A mortgage was applied for from Friends General Conference.

The meetinghouse committee consisted of Paulding Philips, Gretchen Hull, Ernie Foust, Rob Patterson, Nancy Booth, Pete Haviland, and Bill Bowers, with Claire Darrow as clerk. Their first chore was to keep lines of communication open with the whole meeting.

The architectural firm of Lippencott designed the structure. By 6th month 1994, after extensive reviews and revisions of plans, the meeting let bids and contracted with Paul Rodrique of Augusta as the builder.

The groundbreaking was 2nd mo., 3rd, 1995; the building was completed in 5th month. The first meeting for worship was followed by a wedding that same afternoon.

The clerk reports: "It has been an amazing process filled with grace and challenge...it wasn't easy...but all blips and hurdles eventually smoothed out and we were able, as a meeting, to adjust to the limitation of our financial resources imposed on our vision...the process took much longer than we thought, but the end was never really in doubt...now when I approach the meetinghouse, particularly at night, the warm light shines out into the darkness."

The big benches were obtained from the Rockland Red Cross.

SOURCE: *A History of The Meetinghouse Committee of Midcoast Meeting* by Claire Darrow, 1996.

Ralph Greene

Dirigo Friends
Meetinghouse

Dirigo, Maine
Erected: Circa 1840-50
Location: 1/2 mile down the Dirigo/Weeks Mills
**   Road, off Route 3 in China**
Burial Ground: Two nearby
Not in Use as Quaker Meetinghouse

The Dirigo Meetinghouse was a small, crude building built sometime between 1840-50. Rufus Jones (b. 1863) attended there as a small boy. Twice a week the family drove the five miles between their farm and the meeting. Rufus remembered meetings that went on from one to two hours as being for the most part dull except when his aunt and uncle came to visit. The aunt and uncle were Sybil and Eli Jones, founders of the Friends Schools in Ramallah. They also carried their Quaker work to England, Ireland, the Continent, and even once to Africa. The Eli and Sybil Jones house sits on the corner as you turn toward Weeks Mills. Eli and Sybil Jones are buried in a nearby burial ground. The meeting-house was sold in 1891 and is now part of a nearby barn.

SOURCE: Miriam E. Brown, niece of Rufus Jones, New England Yearly Meeting, 1990. Also Ralph Greene, Orland, Maine.

Left: Durham Friends Meetinghouse after renovations.

Below: Durham Friends Meetinghouse (with 1956-57 addition)

Nancy Marstaller

Durham Monthly Meeting of Friends, established 1790 ~ this Meetinghouse (third) built 1829 ~

Durham, Maine

Erected: 1829

Location: Intersection of Route 125 and
**   Quaker Meetinghouse Road**

Burial Ground: Yes

In Use as Quaker Meetinghouse

The first meetings in Durham were held in the home of Joseph Estes; a preparative meeting was formed in 1776, and remained part of Falmouth Monthly Meeting until 1790. In that year Joseph Estes conveyed a deed to three acres at the present site to representatives of the meeting for the sum of two pounds. A house was erected, but by 1799 it was replaced by a larger, two-story frame building measuring forty feet by forty-five feet. In 1828, Waitsill Webber was employed to shingle the foreside of the meeting-house and make what repairs were needed to the same with good materials and in a worklike manner for the sum of $28.00. During the summer

of 1829, this structure burned, presumably from a spark from the blacksmith shop across the street, which was owned by Elisha Tuttle.

A committee from Quarterly Meeting recommended that the burned building be replaced by a brick structure forty feet by sixty feet. The third and present structure, it was completed 12th Month 1829 at a cost of $750.

In its original form the meetinghouse had two sets of double doors at the front, and traditional wooden shutters divided the interior. A double set of facing seats ran along the north wall with enclosed stairs leading to the attic in the back corner. The building was remodeled in 1900 to include a door at one end at a cost of $1,085. An addition was built in 1956-7.

The meeting established a library in 1833, and a missionary committee worked with Native Americans in Kansas beginning in 1899. There is a burial ground and parsonage adjacent to the meetinghouse.

SOURCE: Hattie Cox, Centennial Celebration, 1929.

between Benton and Albion. It is being used as a community church now.

Source: *Sebasticook—Benton, Maine—1842 to 1942* by Chester E. Basford and others. Also Ralph Greene, Orland, Maine.

East Benton Friends Meetinghouse

East Parsonsfield Friends Meetinghouse

East Benton, Maine
Erected: 1900
Location: East Benton Road, just outside of Albion
Burial Ground: No.
No Longer in Use as Quaker Meetinghouse

A Friends Church was built in 1900 in East Benton on land given by Hiram Robinson and wife. The building was made possible through the efforts of Reverend Mark Thomas of Durham Friends Meeting. It was dedicated on 9th month, 10th of that year. The East Benton Meetinghouse is

East Parsonsfield, Maine
Erected: 1877
Location: 5 miles west of Limerick on Route 160 in middle of village
Burial Ground: The old burial ground near the old Cartland farm is overground off Benton Road; it is set off by a wooden fence.
No Longer in Use as Quaker Meetinghouse

The first Friends in Parsonsfield were the Pelatiah Cartland family from Lee, New Hampshire—home of Moses Cartland. The first meeting is believed to have been held in 1798. By 1838 there were a sufficient number of Friends to call for a meetinghouse, which was subsequently built on land belonging to the Cartland family about one-and-a-half miles from East Parsonsfield Village. It was used for about forty years. One tradition is that at a later date this structure became a Quaker hotel that was run by Charles Varney; another versions is that the meetinghouse became part of the new building.

In 11th month 1876, a committee report recommended that a meetinghouse be built in East Parsonsfield Village; a year later, land was bought from Samuel Lougee for $100, and the present structure was erected shortly thereafter. By 1885 the meeting was prospering and had a hundred members.

Repairs, including shingles and siding, were made to the building in 1895. It was struck by lightning in 1900, making further repairs necessary. In 3rd month 1922, a new stove was added. The year following, the property of Sarah Moulton was purchased for a parsonage. In 1925, W. A. Garner made a gift of a bell, which stood in the vestibule and was rung at monthly meeting. Electric lights were added to both the meetinghouse and the parsonage in 1930. This meeting is in the process of being laid down by Falmouth Quarter. East Parsonsfield Meeting is not currently active; the plan is to keep the meetinghouse and maintain some Quaker presence in the area.

SOURCE: Ralph Greene; and *Notes on the History of the Friends Church, East Parsonsfield* by Laura Barr Lougee, May 25, 1968; supplied by Dorothy Bickford, clerk.

Ralph Greene

Leeds Friends Meetinghouse

Leeds, Maine
Erected: very late 1700s
Location: Quaker Hill Road in Leeds, about 3 miles off Route 106
Burial Ground: No
No Longer in Use as Quaker Meetinghouse

A meeting for worship at Leeds, Maine was begun in 1782. This became a preparative meeting under the care of Durham Monthly Meeting in 1811. In 1813 it was set off as Leeds Monthly Meeting, and then in 1880 to Winthrop Monthly Meeting. The meetinghouse sits in a very beautiful area overlooking the Longfellow Mountains of Maine. The building is presently an apple storage building and is in pretty good condition.

Source: New England Yearly Meeting Archives and Ralph Greene, Orland, Maine.

Paul Sinnott

Lewiston Quaker Church on College Street
(Now Trinity Orthodox Presbyterian)

Lewiston, Maine
Erected: 1875
Location: 93 College Street
Burial Ground: Yes; near second site of earlier
meetinghouse
No Longer in Use as Quaker Meetinghouse

Apparently Amos Davis came to Lewiston from Gloucester in 1774 and at his own expense provided a burial ground and erected a small building that was used as both a meetinghouse and a school. Friends built the first regular meetinghouse in 1811 at Vining Place on old Lisbon Road. In 1856 this building was moved to River Road near Isaac Goddard's. An 1873 map shows a burial ground farther north on River Road near a schoolhouse that later became a dwelling. Friends are buried in this burial ground, now owned by the city of Lewiston. The building was torn down in 1875.

A new Friends church was built at 93 College Street, and the first service held there in 8th month 1875. This wood-frame building measures thirty-four feet by fifty-two feet and has a seating capacity of about two hundred and fifty. It was built at a cost of $3,500.

This meeting was laid down in 1911 when the few remaining members were transferred to Durham. The building was sold in 1913 to the First Church Christ Scientist and later to the Trinity Orthodox Presbyterian Church, which continues as its present owner.

SOURCE: Lewiston Town History. Charles Swan.

West Gardner Friends Meetinghouse

Ralph Greene

Manchester Friends Meetinghouse

Litchfield-West Gardner, Maine
Erected: 1813
Location: Intersection of Neck Road, Collins
 Mills Road, and West Road
Burial Ground: No
No Longer in Use as Quaker Meetinghouse

The Leeds Monthly Meeting appointed a committee to help establish Litchfield Meeting in 5th month 1813 and recommended that "A building twenty-six by thirty-six feet with ten foot posts be built near the schoolhouse where they now meet." They later received a donation of $150 for building costs and paid $7.42 for the land. The site of the laid down West Gardner Meetinghouse is now used by another denomination.

SOURCE: *The Illustrated History of Kennebec County.*

Manchester, Maine
Erected: 1837
Burial Ground: No
Private Residence

The meetinghouse was erected at a cost of $985.00 on land formerly owned by John Hawkes. The building was fifty-four feet by forty-two feet with twelve-foot posts. Services were unprogrammed until 1865, when Warren Hawkes delivered an address on Lincoln's assassination that so impressed his listeners that they made him their minister. He served until a few years before his death in 1935 at the age of ninety-nine, after which the meeting was discontinued.

The meeting room had benches on each side facing raised seats on the north wall, as well as dividing shutters that were lowered by cords and pulleys. The first heat was a "potash stove"—essentially a ring of bricks with a large iron kettle inverted over it with spaces for a flue and a door. Business meetings retained both male and female clerks until 1888. Repairs were made in 1884 and a small chimney added. Originally there had been a wooden platform at one end of the building to help people mount and dismount from carriages, and a set of open horse sheds

The building was sold in 1942, and converted to a private residence without substantial changes being made to the exterior. A large central chimney was also added.

SOURCE: From an article placed in the foundation of the new chimney when the meetinghouse was converted to a dwelling in 1942, supplied by Annette Peabody, secretary of Manchester Elementary School. Also Ralph Greene, Orland, Maine.

Former North Berwick Friends Meetinghouse
Elm and Maple Streets

North Berwick, Maine
Erected: 1850
Location: Elm and Maple Streets
Burial Ground: Yes, nearby.
No Longer in Use as Quaker Meetinghouse

North Berwick Friends Meetinghouse (Second)

The first meetinghouse was located on the Oak Woods Road, south of Bonny Bigg. It was built in 1742 and later torn down. The second was at the site of the present Friends cemetery located about a mile south of the village on Route 4. It was built in 1758 and later moved to the village and stood on the site of the present parking lot for the Corner Restaurant. It eventually became a residence and was later razed. A burial ground marker bears the date 1750.

North Berwick Friends Meetinghouse (Third)

The third and present building, which measures sixty-two feet by thirty-six feet, rising to forty feet at the peak, was built at the corner of Elm and Maple Streets.

Originally, there were nine rows of Norwegian walnut and pine benches, a heating stove, and a small balcony at the rear of the meeting room. There was also a second room that served as town library and First Day school. The interior was apparently remodeled about 1900. The building was sold in 1919, although Friends were permitted to use it for several years afterwards. In 1929 James A. Coney, a Friends minister, moved to town and the house was used for meeting again, though most of the attendees were not Friends. James Coney was superintendent of the Orthodox Yearly Meeting of Friends in New England at the time of the 1945 re-unification and served as New England Yearly Meeting's first Field Secretary. After Mr. Coney's departure in 1950, the building was sold for use as a store and remains in commercial use.

SOURCE: Audrey Hett.

North Fairfield Meetinghouse

North Fairfield, Maine
Erected: 1840
Location: On Route 104, 2 ½ miles north of Fairfield Center
Burial Ground: Yes
In Use as Quaker Meetinghouse

The first meeting was organized here in 1784, and the first meetinghouse was a log structure thought to have been located near Martins Stream and Covell Road in what is now Larone. This building burned, and a second log structure was erected at or near the site of the present house. It is reported that the floor of this structure gave way, making a new building necessary.

The present meetinghouse was raised 5th month, 29th, 1838, on land deeded in 1791 by a person named Hoxie. The building itself, a two-story frame clapboard with the general features of Greek revival architecture, was finally finished and dedicated 7th month, 13th, 1840. Unlike many Friends meetinghouses, it has only a single front door. The type of saw marks on the benches indicate that they were cut before circular saws were in use. In 1840 a public school was started in the building, and a horse shed built in that same year stood until 1930.

There is a burial ground in back of the building. In the southeastern corner there is a large boulder marked "1784," which is believed to mark the burial site of earlier Friends who in the mid-1700s occupied a British Crown Land Grant known as the Quaker Tract.

Oak Grove Meetinghouse

Oak Grove, Maine
Erected: 1784
Location:
Burial Ground: yes
No Longer in Use as Quaker Meetinghouse

Originally built in 1784, this meeting was replaced in 1812 and again in 1842. A new chapel was given by Charles Bailey in 1895 and later repaired by his daughter, Eleanor Bailey Woodman. A foundation, walls, and a basement were added to the east end in 1949, along with a

covered porch. New pews were added in 1960, and a parking lot was added in 1961. It is difficult to believe that the present structure, with its steeple and stained glass windows, bears any resemblance to the original. It is now in a general state of neglect. There is an adjoining burial ground.

Present Portland Friends Meetinghouse

Portland, Maine
Erected: 1842-1845
Location: 1837 Forest Avenue
Burial Ground: Yes
In Use as Quaker Meetinghouse

The first meetinghouse in Portland was a small building built in 1752 near the Presumpscot River on the edge of Falmouth. It was replaced by a larger building in 1768, which in turn was replaced by the present building on Forest Avenue. The building was completed in 1845 using some of the timbers from the previous structure. More recently, a full basement with schoolrooms and a modern furnace have been added. There is a large 140 year-old burial ground behind the meetinghouse.

In addition to the present Forest Avenue Meeting, there was formerly a large pastoral meeting on Oak Street. The first house there was dated 1849 but was replaced in 1895 by a larger and more "church-like" structure. This meeting was combined with Forest Avenue in the 1930s. The structure on Oak Street burned in 1970.

St. Albans Friends Meetinghouse

St. Albans, Maine
Erected: N/A
Located: Mason Corner Road
Burial Ground: No
No Longer in Use as Quaker Meetinghouse

St. Albans became a preparative meeting in 1828 and a Monthly Meeting in 1840. It is listed as part of Fairfield Quarter in 1841. It was attached to Winthrop Monthly Meeting in 1928 when it was laid down. The original building (no date) was moved across the street to become a residence and was replaced by the present "church" on the same site. The original steeple on the church is no longer there. The building was purchased by the town in 1955 and is presently in use as the town community house and called The Chatterbox Club.

Portland Friends Meetinghouse, Oak Street, 1849-1895
(Portland Second, pastoral)

Unity Friends Meetinghouse

Unity, Maine
Erected: 1827
Location: Quaker Hill Road beyond Unity
College
Burial Ground: Yes
No Longer in Use as Quaker Meetinghouse

Unity Friends attended a preparative meeting under the care of the China Monthly Meeting, which approved construction of a building thirty feet square and one story high to stand on a one-acre plot owned by Asa Jones. This meetinghouse was built on the crest of Quaker Hill overlooking the valley of Sandy Stream. The builders were Benjamin R. Stevens and Clement Rockcliff, and Asa Jones also gave a lot adjacent to the building for a burial ground.

At Quarterly Meeting in Vassalboro in 1837, Unity Meeting became a Monthly Meeting that included the towns of Albion, Unity, and Brooks.

On 2nd month, 2nd, 1873, the New England Yearly Meeting assembled at Unity and was addressed by Elizabeth Comstock at the Union Church.

Attendance declined after 1910, and by the 1930s only occasional summer meetings were still held.

The meetinghouse still stands on its original site. After being idle for a long time, it was purchased by Gantz Hunter, donated to the community, and reopened as the South Unity Community Church in 1960. It is now in use by a Baptist congregation.

Ruben Brackett was a prominent Unity Quaker. He manufactured clocks and cloth carpets and was the first person to use rubber on fabric. The painting of a codfish that hangs in the Boston House of Representatives is the work of his son Walter, who was said to have done the best oil paintings of fish in America.

SOURCE: *History of the Town of Unity, M*aine by James Berry Vickery III. Falmouth Publishing House, Manchester, Maine, 1954. Additional information supplied by Mrs. Jan Darling, library aid, Unity College.

Vassalboro Friends Meetinghouse

Cobscook Friends Meetinghouse

East Vassalboro, Maine
(Also once called East Pond)
Erected: 1833
Location: East at Four Corners off Route 32
Burial Ground: Yes
In Use as Quaker Meetinghouse

The first meetinghouse in East Vassalboro was a wooden structure built in 1798. Because of its limited size, it was replaced by the present brick meetinghouse. This meeting was the home of John Davis Lang, a Quaker minister who was involved in the founding of Oak Grove-Coburn School. The meeting was unprogrammed until 1890, when it became pastoral, and so continued until 1980, when it returned to unprogrammed worship. There is an associated burial ground.

Whiting, Maine
Erected: 1990
Location: On Route 189 (Lubec Road; meeting
    1/2 mile from beginning of Route 189)
In Use as Quaker Meetinghouse

Whiting, Maine, near the Canadian border, seems an unlikely location for a meeting, yet in 1985, this "acorn" meeting decided it needed its own house. A committee of Ralph Cook, Harry Snyder, Walter Plant, Dr. Francis Schumann, and Mary Goodies initiated and directed the project, which resulted in a twenty-six foot by forty-foot wooden Cape structure built on an acre of land donated by Audry and Harry Snyder.

Loans, gifts of materials, volunteer labor, grants from the Obadiah Brown Benevolent Fund, a yard sale, a work day by the Quarter organized by Andy Grannell, and a ten-dollar donation from an inmate of the Maine State Prison all combined to equal a sum valued well in excess of $35,000.

The new house is seeing increased use; attendance at meeting for worship has about doubled, ranging from twenty to as high as forty. Five benches were acquired from the Purchase (NY) Meeting following a fire there.

SOURCE: From information supplied by Audry Snyder, recorder of Cobscook Monthly Meeting, 9th month, 28th, 1991.

Michael Wozich

Windham Friends Meetinghouse

Windham, Maine
Erected: 1849
Location: Route 202, south of Windham Center
Burial Ground: Yes
In Use as Quaker Meetinghouse

The first Friends Meetinghouse of Windham was erected near Windham Center opposite the residence of the late Nathaniel Cobb on Town Farm Road (now owned by Mrs. Jack Clark and formerly the Walter Reeves family). It was a small, one-story building. Later a two-story addition was built and fitted for an academy.

The present meetinghouse was erected across the field from the first meetinghouse). Stephen Webb, Jr. contracted to build it for $910. The meeting took a loan of $300 for the project. Falmouth Quarterly Meeting paid $210 as their

part toward the new structure.

The new meetinghouse contained some of the old desks and benches that, judging from their age, came from the first meetinghouse. The meeting auctioned off most of these antiques in 1999 to fund major meetinghouse repairs.

The Religious Society of Friends is the next oldest religious society in Windham. Quakers began meeting for "Publick Worship" in 1779. A preparative meeting (1793) became a monthly meeting in 1803. It is the only religious society in Windham to sustain public worship from its first organization to the present.

Today Windham Friends Meeting has a small membership, but a wide circle of sincere and interested people attend and support the meeting.

Source: Michael Wozich, clerk of Windham Friends Meeting.

Winthrop, Maine
Erected: 1880s
Location: Route 135, South of Route 202
Burial Ground: 3/4 mile south of church
In Use as Quaker Meetinghouse

The first regular meeting for worship was in 1793. The first meetinghouse was on land owned by Stewart Foster, on a site opposite the present structure. It was warmed by a "potash kettle"—a stove consisting of a built-up ring of bricks topped by a large inverted kettle. The meeting soon outgrew the small structure, which was sold as a blacksmith shop.

The second meetinghouse, built on the site of the present one, was twenty-four feet by thirty feet long. By 1883, this proved too small. It was sold as a dwelling and was replaced by the present building—a large Friends church of Gothic revival style, replete with bell tower and stained glass windows. Charles Bailey, an early

Winthrop Village Friends Meetinghouse

Winthrop Friends Meetinghouse

manufacturer of linoleum, is said to have paid for the building. One of the more prominent past members was Hannah Bailey, a noted suffragette and temperance leader. The town maintains an associated cemetery, Lakeview, located three-quarters of a mile south of the "church."

SOURCE: *The Illustrated History of Kennebec County*, Henry D. Kingsbury and Simon L. Deyo, editors. H.W. Blake Co., New York, 1892. Original materials contributed by Rufus M. Jones. Supplied by Mary E. Jones.

Winthrop Village, Maine
Erected: circa 1883
Location: Bowdoin Street
Burial Ground: No
No Longer in Use as Quaker Meetinghouse

This structure was used as a Friends church until 1911 when it was laid down. It was then the local high school until 1930, and is presently in use by a Masonic group.

SOURCE: Mary E. Jones and Maggie Edmondson, Winthrop, Maine.

Maine Meetinghouses No Longer Standing

Albion-Fairfax, Maine

A preparative meeting existed in 1812 and had a meetinghouse, but there is no record about the building. The meeting was called Albion after 1824 and became part of Unity Monthly Meeting in 1860. The last members were transferred to Unity in 1884, the year it was laid down. Notes say that the meetinghouse was repaired in 1867.

Athens, Maine

There is no record of a building in this location, though a meeting was established in 1805 and laid down in 1826.

Bristol-Broad Cove, Maine

The first presence of Friends was recorded here in 1784, when a group asked the town if it could be excused from the regular church tax. A meeting for worship was organized in 1795 at the home of Isaac Lincoln. By 1798 the group was strong enough to erect a small meetinghouse with adjacent burial ground on land purchased from George Rhodes. This became a preparative meeting in 1801. After the meeting ceased in 1826 the meetinghouse gradually decayed and was finally taken down. The cemetery remains under the care of Vassalboro Monthly Meeting.

SOURCE: *History of the Towns of Bristol and Bremen, Maine* by John Johnston, 1873 (pages 395 and 428).

Cape Elizabeth, Maine

Archival records indicate the existence of a Quaker worship group as early as 1782 and a meetinghouse built in 1814. The local history reports that "Quakers built a small plain unpainted Meetinghouse in what is now Bayview Cemetery on Sawyer Street about 1828. The building was used for Town Meetings in the years 1835 to 1837. Two prominent members were Nathaniel Dyer and Greely Hannaford. The meetinghouse was sold about 1865 to Captain John W. Burke and moved to a new location. Quakers are buried in the old section. (The cemetery has since been renamed and is a private association.)"

SOURCE: *A History of Cape Elizabeth, Maine* by William B. Jordan, Jr., 1965.

Falmouth, Maine

The first Friends settled in Falmouth about 1743. Among them were families such as the Winslows, Morrells, Allens, Halls, and Goddards, who occupied land along the Persumpscot River. A small meetinghouse was built in 1751-52 near Blackstrap Road. This was replaced in 1768 with a larger building measuring thirty-two by forty feet and a burying ground on an acre of land on the south side of the river.

In 1774 Quakers were exempted from paying parish taxes in support of a minister. By 1790 a meeting was allowed in Portland proper, and in 1796 a two-story brick house, thirty-six by forty feet, was erected on the corner of Federal and Pearl Streets.

In March 1842, according to some reports, the

cemetery was "full" and the meetinghouse was noted to be in "dilapidated condition." In July of 1842, the meetinghouse was noted to be "beyond repair"; a committee was appointed to find a new location and build another. In 1847, a new meetinghouse was built on Forest Avenue in Portland. Some timbers from the old building were used in its construction.

SOURCE: Materials supplied by the Falmouth Public Library, including a copy of the deed to the first meetinghouse site.

Gorham, Maine

Friends in Gorham held a preparative meeting in private homes as early as 1777. In 1805 Friends built a meetinghouse for $300 in the Horton district of Gorham on land of Jedehiah Cobb. The building measured thirty by thirty feet and stood on the corner of Huston Road and Harding Bridge Road. Meeting for worship was a 11 a.m. on Sundays and Wednesdays. The first important Quaker minister to visit from out of the area was Mary Baker from Nantucket.

Membership declined and those left transferred to nearby Windham Friends Meeting. The meetinghouse was sold in 1849 and moved to Bracket Road in the Little Falls area, which is located on the western edge of town. The building was used as a dwelling. It has not been determined whether it is still standing.

There is no record of a Friends burying ground. One tradition is that the bodies of two Friends were removed from Gorham to the Friends cemetery in Windham.

Source: Information from McLellan's *History of Gorham*

(1903) and from Baxter Memorial Library, with special thanks to George L. Watson, archivist of the Gorham Historical Society.

Hope-Appleton, Maine

The Friends meetinghouse stood in what is called the Quaker burying ground. In 1868 the building was removed from the cemetery and became part of Stephen Simmons's house. Sixty-five years later fire destroyed the entire structure.

SOURCE: *Appleton Register 195?*, issued by the Appleton Community Club. Maine Historical Society call number MX AP 53.3.

Marker in Eliot reads as follows:
"The site of the First Quaker Meeting House in Maine, built in Dover, N.H., taken down and reerected here in 1769"

Kittery-Eliot, Maine

The first meeting in Maine was in Kittery in late 12th month 1662. Ann Coleman, Mary Tompkins, and Alice Ambrose were three "publishers of truth" driven out by Sheriff Waldron.

Kittery, at that time included Eliot (1810), Berwick (1714), and South Berwick (1814), the combined area being called the Piscataqua District.

Thomas Frothingale, a Philadelphia Friend, reports going to meeting in 4th month 1721 in Kittery and Portsmouth. The Kittery Town Book of 1732 lists a substantial number of Quakers; a law passed in 1728 allowed Episcopalians, Baptists, and Quakers to pay their own church assessments. Parson Wise recorded the baptism in 1716 of one Mary Foss, "wonderfully recovered from the Quakers."

Quakers are also reported as going to meeting in Dover, New Hampshire, and there was an established meeting in upper Eliot in 1730.

So far, no record has surfaced of a meetinghouse in Kittery, Portsmouth, or Eliot before 1769, when the 1680 house from Dover Neck was taken apart and re-erected in Eliot at the corner of what are now State and River Roads. There is a bronze plaque marking the site on what is said to have been a carriage stone once used as a horse block for dismounting. An 1880 history notes that "a large Society still exists in North Berwick where their (Eliot) worship was subsequently transferred."

SOURCE: *History of York County, 1889—Its Prominent Men And Pioneers*, Everts and Beck, Philadelphia publishers. *History of the Old Town of Berwick* by Sarah Orne Jewett, no date. Also, *Old Kittery and Her Families* by Everett Stackpole, 1903.

Limington Friends Meetinghouse

Limington, Maine

This meeting is now the Lewiston Monthly Meeting, and meets in Lewiston at a site near Bates College. The original meetinghouse in Limington was built by Samuel Brackett in 1807, then rebuilt and reduced in size in 1858. Meetings were continued until 1887, when the building was sold to the Bullockites Friends, then to Parsonsfield Meeting. Mr. Westover, a local orchard operator in his nineties, reported that the building was removed to East Waterboro where it was incorporated into a local church. Another tradition is that the building was taken to South Waterboro where it was destroyed by forest fires in 1947.

Pownal, Maine

The Pownal Meetinghouse was built in 1800, two miles east of Pownal Center opposite the then home of Simon Estes. The road was once called "Quaker Road" because Quaker families named Estes, Austin, Pote, and Goddard lived along it.

SOURCE: *History of Pownal* by Ettie Latham, 1908.

Sidney Friends Meetinghouse

Sidney, Maine

The building in the picture above was located at the junction of Quaker and Robinson Roads. It is the second Sidney house. The first was erected some time between 1802, when the Sidney meeting was split off from Vassalboro, and 1806, when the deed to the land (an acre lot on the west side of Quaker Road) on which it stood was obtained from Jeremiah Butler. At the same time, a half-acre on the east side of the road was purchased for a burying ground.

The second house was built in 1857 about a mile south of the original lot, which was sold to William Purington for $8.00. This second house was laid down in 1933. There is a cemetery on the property, and at one time there were horse sheds to the rear of the meetinghouse. In 1939 Chester Freeman sold the property to Gladys Cummings for $50; the money was turned over to the Winthrop Monthly Meeting per a receipt witnessed by Arthur Jones on 5th month, 29th, 1938.

Mrs. Cummings removed the podium as agreed and leased the building to her son-in-law, who operated it as a dance hall. Although it burned in 1942, local lore has it that not everyone liked having a Quaker Church used as a dance hall.

There is a local poem titled, "Quaker Church On Quaker Hill" by Mary Freeman Philbrick.

SOURCE: Donald Freeman, Bradford, Massachusetts.

Thorndike, Maine

The town clerk believes that many years ago there was a meetinghouse on Files Hill, but there is no land marker or record of any kind to verify its existence.

SOURCE: By letter dated November 1986.

Quaker Burial Grounds in Maine

Bristol-Broad Cove, Maine—

Adjacent to site of meeting; under care of Vassalboro Monthly Meeting.

Brooks, Maine—

On Route 7 (Moose Head Trail) on way to Woods Jackson.

Cape Elizabeth, Maine—

On Sawyer Street; Quakers are buried in old section. Burial ground is now under care of a private association.

Casco, Maine—

Two; both are near meetinghouse on Quaker Ridge Road.

China and South China, Maine—

There are six scattered Quaker burial grounds, three under the care of the town and three under the care of China Monthly Meeting. Of these last three, one is located on Village Street, one is on Lakeview Road, and one is on China Neck Road on the northwest side of China Lake, looking from China.

Durham, Maine—

Adjacent to meetinghouse at the intersection of Route 125 and Quaker Meetinghouse Road.

East Parsonsfield, Maine—

Old burial ground near the old Cartland farm is off Benton Road. It is set off by a wooden fence.

Falmouth, Maine—

Burial ground is on Blackstrap Road near site of earliest Falmouth meetinghouse.

Hope-Appleton, Maine—

The Quaker Cemetery is located on the west side of East Sennebec Road, about one-half mile from the town office.

Lewiston, Maine—

North of later meetinghouse site on River Road. Burial ground reputed to be in disrepair.

North Berwick, Maine—

A mile south of village on Route 4, at original site of second meetinghouse.

North Fairfield, Maine—

On Route 104, 2 1/2 miles north of Fairfield Center, to rear of meetinghouse.

Portland, Maine—

1837 Forest Avenue, behind the meetinghouse.

Sidney, Maine—

1) On east side of Quaker Road, across from site of first meetinghouse;

2) approximately one mile south of first meetinghouse site; now on private property.

Unity, Maine—

Adjacent to building on Quaker Hill Road beyond Unity College.

Vassalboro, Maine—

1) On Route 201 in Vassalboro, adjacent to Oak Grove Meetinghouse;

2) adjacent to Vassalboro Friends Meetinghouse, east at Four Corners off Route 32.

Windham, Maine—

Adjacent to meetinghouse on Route 202, south of Windham Center.

Winthrop, Maine—

Called "Lakeview," the burial ground is three-quarter miles south of meetinghouse on Route 135, south of Route 202.

Massachusetts

Massachusetts

There are more meetinghouses in Massachusetts than in other New England states. In fact, there are so many that it is hard to decide where to begin. Since no one point seems better than another, I'll start with Cape Cod.

A generous set of materials on South Yarmouth was provided to me by Michael Preston, who also sent photos of the South Yarmouth meetinghouse and burying ground. Besides the present meetinghouse plot, there remains a small burying ground near the upper end of the Bass River off Mayfair Road in Dennis, which was the site of the first meetinghouse, built in 1714. The present one was built in 1809, laid down in 1909, and reopened in 1954. The grounds contain a small schoolhouse built elsewhere in the early 1820s as a Quaker village school and now used for First Day School.

In connection with this meeting I am especially indebted to Barbara R. Ditmars for extensive background information, not only about the building past and present, but also about important Quaker family associations with the South Yarmouth meeting. Laurence Barber, a Quaker historian, has documented the names of all those who were buried in the cemetery and has done an extensive history of Friends in the South Yarmouth area.

Two other meetinghouses are located on the Cape—one in East Sandwich, and one in West Falmouth. Cape historian James W. Gould reports that an important Quaker home, built in 1641, may be found near the present Sandwich Meetinghouse. Owned by the Wing family, it contains a great deal of important Quaker memorabilia and is open to the public. Gould notes that a Quaker carpenter named Samuel Dottridge, whose 1790 house in Scituate is now maintained by the town's historical society, used to walk ten miles each way to attend meeting in Sandwich. The Sandwich Meetinghouse is referred to as "the Great Meetinghouse" because of its size. The present house (the third structure to be erected on the same site) was built in 1810. It measures forty-eight feet by thirty-six feet and is two stories high. It is located on Spring Hill.

The third extant meetinghouse on the Cape is in West Falmouth, where Quakers settled early, perhaps in part because it was the first town in America to exempt Quakers from the church tax.

Three hundred and fifty feet east of the meetinghouse is the oldest recorded Quaker graveyard on the Cape; it is marked by a boulder that was put in place in 1900. The old fieldstones previously used as markers were removed and replaced by new stones in 1888.

The history of this meeting is set forth in a bulletin celebrating the meeting's 300th anniversary—"Quakers in West Falmouth 1685 to 1985." The first meetinghouse, completed in 1725, was thirty feet square and had a triangular hopper roof with a hole in the peak to let the smoke out from the charcoal used for heating. Contrary to some legends about our sturdy ancestors, early Friends were just as interested in keeping warm as we are today. The site of the structure is marked with a stone bearing the letters FMH. The structure was enlarged in 1794 but became too small by 1842, when it was torn down. The frame was removed to South Yarmouth where it became a frame of Quaker David Kelley's barn.

The Pembroke meetinghouse is of special interest in that it is one of only three in the state that have been deemed of sufficient historic importance to have had funds provided by the state historic preservation commission for restoration. The state provided $38,500 that was matched by the town. The plea for town funds did not fall on deaf ears when Elizabeth Bates of the town historic commission said: "We talk about quality of life in our town....this building is part of our heritage and a valuable historic relic dating 175 years before the Statue of Liberty—if we can build a $40,000 dog pound, we can do this (i.e., match the state grant). The local paper carried the headline, "The Quaker Meetinghouse, A Home With No More Friends." Sub-head: "Abandoned By Its Own Society." An earlier restoration effort made by an individual with local Quaker ancestors had prompted a headline that read "Last Of Quaker Colony Awaits Church Decay."

Local history notes that in early colonial times, in a conflict between the local Congregationalists and the Quakers, a particularly factious lawyer repeatedly attacked the leading local Friend, a mild-tempered person. One day the Friend appeared with a boatload of fish and the lawyer said, "Friend Wanton, you are like the apostle Peter. In the first place, he was a fisherman and so are you. Secondly, he was a preacher and so are you. And thirdly, he denied the Lord and so do you." It just happened that Friend Wanton had just given all the fish he'd just caught to a group that was having a party.

Swansea meeting suffered a series of conflicts among its members, resulting in a split in 1844 between the followers of John Wilbur and those of another mind. Thomas Wilbur, clerk and nephew of John Wilbur, refused to give up his position and turn over the meeting minutes to a new clerk, who had been appointed by the New England Yearly Meeting because it had not been notified of any new officers for a number of years. It wasn't until twenty years later that the records were surrendered. They are now in the New England Yearly Meeting Archives in Providence, Rhode Island.

Virginia Morrison, librarian for Allen's Neck, sent me information about the famous clambake this meeting has annually to raise funds. She enclosed a photo taken in 1959 of meeting members gathered in front of the house, and identified Ernest Weed in the front row. Ernest and his wife were managers of Beacon Hill Friends House.

Tracing the whereabouts of the former West Newbury meetinghouse led me in a most unexpected direction. Folks at the local library suggested that a local resident, Spencer Ordway, would be able to provide me with more information than they could. He was indeed very helpful, but expressed concern about the condition of the meeting's burying ground located on Turkey Hill. He and some others had tried to care for it, but it was now full of broken stones and trash. Mr. Ordway furnished me with a record of the burials there, a list that included many Sawyer family members. I checked with the town selectmen about the care of the place, and found that no provisions had ever been made. They were, however, most cooperative about cleaning up some of the worst of the mess. The Sawyer Family Association was also concerned about the problem but didn't seem to have any funds to help.

Little remains of the Religious Society of Friends in Salem except for a well-kept and well-marked burying ground. At one time, Friends were considered as much of a menace to good order as witches later were. In 1694 Friend Thomas Maule published a book entitled *Truth Held Forth and Maintained*, which explained and defended views held by Quakers. The governor and council directed the sheriff to search Maule's house and burn all copies of the offending work. Maule was arrested for publishing a book "wherein is contained divers slanders against churches and the government of this Province."

Sometimes whole meetings were a source of trouble. A note records that in 1821 the Richmond overseers of the Pelham preparative meeting "Removed its preparative status for having difficulty for keeping this meeting in the authority of the truth."[1] When I went to look for the site of this meeting, the superintendent of public works in Amherst advised me of the location of its former and largely lost cemetery. After an unsuccessful first try and a second visit with him, Constance and I finally did locate a few stones lost in the woods.

Apponegansett Friends in South Dartmouth decided to build a meetinghouse in 1698—"For the people of God, in scorn, called Quakers, thirty-five foot long and thirty foot wide with fourteen-foot studs to worship and serve the loving God as in Conscience they ought to do." A pot of coal for heating purposes was installed in 1710. The present building has a date of 1790.

My first acquaintance with the Bolton Meetinghouse occurred a number of years before I started this project. I discovered it on a visit to the Old Sturbridge Village Museum, where it had been moved from its former site in Bolton and re-erected under an arrangement made through the Smithfield Quarterly Meeting in 1952. Bolton Friends raised $4,000 to match the $4,000 raised by Sturbridge Village. Reassembled in 1954, it was formally dedicated on 9th month, 2nd.

Given the date of the house, 1797, I was convinced that something was wrong, because the structure has no dividing partition or movable panels such as were used when men's and women's business meetings were held separately. In 1818 an addition of twenty feet was added and it was recorded that "A partition (was) added also to separate men's and women's business meetings." Unfortunately, when the building was removed to Sturbridge Village, the center section with the divider was not included. Thus, the restored building does not accurately reflect eighteenth-century Quaker meetinghouses.

One of the most interesting facts about the Westport's second and greatly altered meetinghouse is that Paul Cuffe was on the building committee. Cuffe was a famous black Quaker merchant and friend of Dolley Madison, who was also a Quaker. She arranged for him to meet with her husband, President James Madison, over a trade concern Cuffe had.

In the minutes of the Uxbridge meeting, an item entitled "Sleeping In Our Religious Meetings" relates to those who fell asleep: "If they be such as have usually have sat facing the meeting, whether they be elders, ministers, or others, let them withdraw from such seats that their ill example and reproach be lessened and take seats with members at large until they and friends are sensible of an overcoming."

The Rules of Discipline were applied to all, regardless of status, and without fear or favor. Stephen Hopkins, chief justice of the state supreme court, governor of the state, member of the Continental Congress, and signer of the Declaration of Independence was berated repeatedly for keeping a female slave. When he refused to grant her freedom, he was finally read out of meeting.

In Lawrence, a building constructed in 1895 is an outstanding example of a Friends structure in southern New England that is architecturally representative of a period when pastoral (or programmed) Friends were in ascendancy and built churches instead of the traditional unadorned meetinghouses.

During that period, similar structures would have been found in Roxbury, Worcester, and Fall River. A greatly modified form in Lynn also still stands; like the one in Lawrence, it is presently used by another religious denomination. There are other Quaker church buildings still standing in Maine, including ones in Lewiston, Winthrop, and Oak Grove.

Allen Sifferlen, in writing me about the meetinghouse in Lawrence, said: "I believe that the building has importance in showing the Quaker influence to simplify, order, and restrain the ecclesiastical architecture and ecclesiasticism of the late nineteenth century." The building stands today in its original form, almost completely unaltered.

The history of Friends on Nantucket Island is dramatic. The first meeting was formed in 1708. In the years that followed, a meetinghouse at the corner of

Pleasant and Main Streets served fifteen hundred; it had to be enlarged in 1762 to accommodate the twenty-four hundred Quakers then on the island. After 1820, numbers declined rapidly. The meeting broke into three sects—the Hicksites, Gurneyites, and Wilburites—all with different houses. By 1860 there were only a few Quakers left on the island, and by 1900 there were none—a sad commentary. Today a Friends worship group meets in the Quaker meetinghouse on Fair Street, now owned by the Nantucket Historical Society.

[1]See *Disowned, Disrupted, Dissolved: The Life and Times of the Members of the Society of Friends, (Quakers) in Pelham, Massachusetts, 1806-1870* by Paul Bigelow, 1985.

Massachusetts Meetinghouses

Adams Friends Meetinghouse

Adams, Massachusetts
Erected: 1782
Location: Friends Street
Burial Ground: Yes
No Longer in Use as Quaker Meetinghouse
National Register of Historic Buildings

The town of Adams was settled about 1769 by Quakers from Smithfield, Rhode Island and Dartmouth, Massachusetts. They first met in the home of Isaac Killey.

The land on which the meetinghouse stands and the large adjoining burial ground, now used by the town, were conveyed to the meeting in 1797 by Isaac Killey, John and Patience Lapham, John Russell, and James Lapham. This twenty-eight by thirty-six-foot, two-story structure is among the finest untouched meetinghouses in New England. It remains in its original form. The interior framing of oak and pine is fully exposed, and the original benches remain in place. Two rather delicate octagonal posts help support the surrounding gallery, which contains its own fireplace off the main chimney. There is also a large fireplace on the ground floor. The clapboarding on the exterior was redone in 1988.

This building is on the National Register of Historical Landmarks, and is open to the public from 1:00 to 4:00 from Memorial Day through Labor Day. It is under the care of The Society of Friends Descendants. Daniel Anthony, the father of Susan B. Anthony, pioneer worker for women's rights, belonged to this meeting until the family moved to New York when Susan was six years old.

The road past the meetinghouse, now Friends Street, was originally an Indian trail that connected with the famous Mohawk Trail. This meeting was laid down after about sixty years, when there was a large migration of Quakers into New York State.

SOURCE: *The East Hoosick Quaker Meetinghouse,* published in 1992 by the Adams Historical Commission.

Amesbury Friends Meetinghouse

Amesbury, Massachusetts
Erected: 1850
Location: Corner of Friends and Greenleaf
Streets
Burial Ground: Yes
In Use as Quaker Meetinghouse

The first meetinghouse in Amesbury was erected in 1705 on a site near that occupied by the "old number eight mill" on the land of Thomas Bernard. Local selectman Thomas Challes was on the building committee. The second house was erected in 1803-04 on Friends Street on a site now occupied by the Sacred Heart Church.

Famous nineteenth-century Quaker poet John Greenleaf Whittier was clerk of the building committee for the third meetinghouse, a Greek revival style white-frame structure. The carpenter in charge was Thomas W. Thorndike of Weare, New Hampshire. It has dividing shutters down the center and a small balcony to the rear. Large multi-light windows (sixteen over twenty sash) give beautiful interior light. Today the benches are

arranged in an open square. In keeping with Quaker frugality, the small decorative panels on the benches appear only on the end that used to face the aisle.

John Greenleaf Whittier and his family attended the meeting long before they moved to Amesbury. Often he was one of the group that traveled over the road from the Haverhill homestead every First Day and Fifth Day to meeting with Amesbury Friends in worship. In 1836 he came to live in a one-story house across from the meetinghouse of that day on Friend Street. He was accompanied by his mother, his aunt, Mercy Hesse, and his sister, Elizabeth H. Whittier. Although he was away from Amesbury a great deal, when at home he regularly attended the Friends meeting, taking his accustomed seat well forward in the meeting room.

This meeting was laid down in the early 1980s and transferred to New England Yearly Meeting. The meeting was reopened by a small worship group, who rehabilitated it and installed modern facilities. Whittier and other members of his family are buried in the nearby Friends burial ground, which is now part of the larger town cemetery.

Some of the ministers of the Religious Society of Friends who have been associated with the present structure include: Moses Huntington, Mercy S. Davis, Stephen Swett, Gertrude Whittier Cartland, Charles H. Jones, H. Elizabeth Jones, George L. Jones, A. Edward Kelsey, and James Wild.

SOURCE: Ronald Woodwall and Cynthia Fisk; Marion B. Kelsey, M. Jane Davis, and Charles Wiggin.

Boston Meetinghouse (1710-1825) 33-35 Congress Street, at the corner of Quaker Lane, Boston, Massachusetts.

Milton Place Meetinghouse (1831-1865, off Federal Street (at the rear of 100 Summer Street.), Boston, Massachusetts.

Townsend Street Meetinghouse in Roxbury (1894-1926)

Cambridge Friends Meetinghouse (present Boston)

Boston/Cambridge, Massachusetts
Erected: 1937
Location: 5 Longfellow Park, Cambridge
Burial Ground: No
In Use as Quaker Meetinghouse

Boston's first Friends meetinghouse, built in 1695, was located on Brattle Street. It measured twenty by twenty-four feet and was soon outgrown. A second house on what was then called Leverett's Lane (later 35 Congress Street) was built of brick in 1710. This brick meetinghouse was two stories high, measured thirty by thirty-five feet and had a burial ground adjoining it. This building was torn down in 1829.

A new brick building, forty by sixty feet, was completed in May 1831 on Milton Place, just off Federal Street, for the total cost of $17,323.14 for land and building. By 1852, when there was no longer a single resident Friend in the city of Boston, extensive repairs for this third meetinghouse were required. The property was eventually disposed of in 1865 by sale at public auction.

Quakerism in Boston went through a period of renewal in the late 1800s as a result of the "evangelistic labor" of Friends of the pastoral tradition. A new "place of worship for progressive Friends" was built on Townsend Street in Roxbury. Queen Anne in style, it measured sixty feet by sixty feet and had a sixty-foot tower and stained glass windows. It was dedicated 10th month, 28th, 1894. In 1926 it was sold to the Congregational Church Union, together with the pastor's residence and the building that had housed the John Woolman Community Center.

In 1926, with the closing of the Roxbury Meetinghouse, Boston and Cambridge Friends held joint meetings for worship in Cambridge. Ten years later, incorporated as Friends Meeting at Cambridge, Friends acquired the Georgian-style brick house built by Longfellow's daughter, the "laughing Allegra" of his poem "The Children's Hour" at Longfellow Park in Cambridge. The current meetinghouse was built in 1937 on an adjacent lot; Rufus Jones gave the dedication talk at the first meeting for worship, held on 12th month, 5[th.]

SOURCE: *Quakers in Boston, 1656 to 1964* by George A. Selleck, published by the Friends Meeting in Cambridge, 1980.

Beacon Hill, Boston, Massachusetts
Erected: 1804
Location: 6 Chestnut Street
Burial Ground: No
In Use as Quaker Meetinghouse; also includes
 Residential Center

The twin Federal style brick townhouses that constitute Beacon Hill Friends House were built originally for Charles Paine. Number Eight was later occupied by Rose Lathrop, daughter of Nathaniel Hawthorne. Number Six, which was turned into a lodging house in the late 1800s, was purchased by Edward

Beacon Hill Friends Center
and Meetinghouse

Greene in 1910 and restored by Boston architect, William Chester Chase. About ten years later Greene bought Number Eight from his neighbors the Graves sisters and, with the help of Chase, joined the two houses. Chase removed most of the first floor at No. 8 to create a large ballroom, which now serves as the meeting room, and built a library on the second floor.

After the death of Mrs. Greene in 1955, her son, John Gardner Greene, offered the building with its contents and an endowment. A Quaker board was set up and incorporated to accept the property. It has been used by Friends ever since. Beacon Hill Friends House also houses a residential program in community living for college students and a wide age-range of adults in transition.

SOURCE: *Beacon Hill Friends House and its Neighbors.* Also Matthew Martin, director.

Apponegansett Friends Meetinghouse

Theo P. Chase

South Dartmouth, Massachusetts
Erected: 1790
Location: Russell's Mill road, South Dartmouth
Burial Ground: Yes
In Use as Quaker Meetinghouse

The first meetinghouse in Apponegansett was completed in 6th month 1699, and stood on Russell Mills Road. A committee consisting of Peleg Slocum, Jacob Mott, and Abraham and John Tucker had declared on 11th month, 6th, 1698, "To build a Meeting House thirty-five feet long, thirty feet wide with fourteen foot studs for the people in God, in scorn called Quakers." Two weighty Friends, Thomas Story and Roger Gill, reportedly attended the first service in the new house. The meeting prospered and the building was enlarged three times—in 1702, 1727, and 1743. In 1710, heat was installed when William Soule was instructed to "procure a pot and make a fire and coals to burn it in."

The original building was torn down in 1790

and replaced by the present structure, which has a stone fireplace at each end. It is furnished with plain benches and a cedar dividing shutter. This meetinghouse played an unusual role in the early 1920s, when it was used as the set for the Quaker wedding in the film *Down to the Sea in Ships*, starring Clara Bow, the "it" girl. Many local Friends and neighbors were involved as bit players.

The adjoining burial ground was first laid out in 1706; it was enlarged in 1753.

Apponegansett Friends Meeting burial ground

SOURCE: From materials furnished by Philip Cornell and supplied by Fred Allen, pastor of Smith Neck Meeting.

Allen's Neck Friends Meetinghouse

South Dartmouth, Massachusetts
Erected: 1761
Location: 739 Horseneck Road
Burial Ground: No
In Use as Quaker Meetinghouse

Construction of Allen's Neck Meetinghouse was started in 1758, on land donated by Daniel Howland. By 1873 more room was required, and a new building was erected and later enlarged. Along with Smith Neck and Apponogansett, Allen's Neck was a part of Dartmouth Monthly Meeting until it became a monthly meeting itself in 1950.

Allen's Neck Meeting is known especially for the clambakes held to raise funds for the First Day School, a tradition begun in 1888 and continued to this day. The Meeting purchased a nearby grove in 1959 as a permanent place to hold them.

SOURCE: *A Historical Sketch of Allen's Neck Meeting,* furnished by Virginia Morrison.

Smith Neck Friends Meetinghouse (at right)

South Dartmouth, Massachusetts
Erected: 1819
Location: 594 Smith Neck Road
Burial Ground: No
In Use as Quaker Meetinghouse

Smith Neck Friends began to hold Meeting for Worship in members' homes beginning in 1768. A deed of land, dated 12th month, 22nd, 1822 was made to Smith Neck Friends by Caleb Anthony for a meetinghouse site at the corner of Smith Neck Road and Rock O'Dundee Road.

The meetinghouse originally had the traditional two doors and interior dividing partition, but between 1890 and 1900 the double doors were replaced by a single door and vestibule, and the meetinghouse itself was turned from its original position. About this time the meeting became pastoral, and the first paid minister was Edward Wood, who also served the communities of Allen's Neck and Westport. Special midweek meetings were also conducted by an African-American evangelist from Ohio named Noah McLane.

SOURCE: *James Wilcox's Smith's Neck Friends Anniversary —Passing Of The Deed*, furnished by Fred Allen, former pastor, Smith's Neck Friends Meeting.

North Dartmouth Friends Meetinghouse

Deerfield, Massachusetts (moved from North Dartmouth)
Erected: 1849
Location: Originally corner of Route 6 and Tucker Road, North Dartmouth; now at

Woolman Hill Quaker Conference Center, Keets Road, Deerfield, Massachusetts
Burial Ground: Two in North Dartmouth— on Chase Road where Old Westport Road enters; and on Tucker Road
No Longer in Use as Quaker Meetinghouse

The first major meetinghouse in the North Dartmouth area was the Apponegansett Meetinghouse on Russell Mills Road, built in 1699. (See description of Apponegansett Meetinghouse.)

Two early meetinghouses in the area—the Newtown Meetinghouse on Faunce Corner Road, erected in 1754, and one at One Tucker Road, erected in 1828 near the present Gidley School, no longer stand.

The North Dartmouth Meetinghouse stood on land in the Smith Mills area of Dartmouth purchased from Perry Gifford. It was built by the firm of Allen and Williston for the sum of $592.50. The building was enlarged in 1897, when the vestibule was widened and a roofed porch was added. Originally two slate-roofed carriage sheds, with six stalls and a privy in each, stood nearby. The last shed was taken down in 1985 and sold to Dougless of Westport for restoration.

The last meeting for worship in this meetinghouse was held on 9th month, 22nd, 1996. The building was later carefully disassembled, all parts being carefully marked. The building is to be re-erected on a new foundation at the Woolman Hill Quaker Conference Center at Deerfield, Massachusetts in June, 2001. Steve Tyson of Warwick, R.I., who dismantled the meetinghouse at its original site in North Dartmouth, will oversee the rebuilding. The meetinghouse will accommodate one hundred people. Mark Fraser, co-executive director of Woolman Hill Conference Center, says that the meetinghouse will be used for worship and for additional conference space when the center is hosting groups.

There are two Friends burial grounds still in North Dartmouth, one on Chase Road, on land given by Benjamin Tucker, and another on Tucker Road on land donated by the Wilber family.

SOURCE: *The New England Friend* newsletter, Spring 1997, and Ruth Burgess.

West Falmouth Friends Meetinghouse

West Falmouth, Massachusetts
Erected: 1725
Location: Route 28 South from Bourne Bridge to
Thomas Landers Road; south on Route 28A,
1 ½ miles, meetinghouse on right
Burial Ground: Yes
In Use as Quaker Meetinghouse

Quakers settled early in West Falmouth, perhaps because it was the first town in colonial America to exempt Quakers from the tax required from religious groups who dissented from the established church at the time. A Quaker meeting was founded in West Falmouth in 1685 under the care of Sandwich Monthly Meeting and became a separate meeting in 1709. In July 1720, Sandwich Monthly Meeting decided that a meetinghouse should be built at West Falmouth. Ten Sandwich Friends contributed eight of the forty-four pounds subscribed for it, and the first recorded meeting was held on 6th month, 2nd, 1725. This meeting-house stood between what are now Routes 28 and 28A near the town's first Quaker burial ground (used until 1775), on the hill east of the present meeting house off Blacksmith Shop Road. Reportedly measuring thirty feet square, its triangular hopper roof had a hole in the center to allow the smoke from the charcoal fire to escape. (Contrary to legends about our sturdy ancestors, early Friends were just as interested in keeping warm as we are today.) The site is now marked "FMH 1720" on a stone post.

To accommodate a growing membership, the second West Falmouth meetinghouse was built on land given by Richard Lake. Enlarged in 1794, it was torn down in 1842 to make way for the even larger present building. Its frame was transported by barge to South Yarmouth, where it became the frame of Friend David Kelley's barn.

Moses Swift built the present meetinghouse in 1842, and in 1861 Stephen Dillingham built the carriage house across the street for all of $170. In 1894 the interior of the meetinghouse was modernized to reflect the needs of the pastoral Friends who used it then. A wood-burning furnace replaced wood stoves, and the plain benches and facing seats were removed. Dark wainscoting and church-like pews were installed, along with a moveable platform at the front of the room, and the balconies were enclosed for Sunday school and meals. Running water was not added until 1964. Though a strong pastoral program in the early 1900s brought renewed vitality, the meeting gradually declined until new attendees founded an unprogrammed meeting in 1964.

From 1962 to the early 1990s the building was shared with the Falmouth Unitarian Fellowship. In 1969 the meeting acquired the building located on about two acres of land behind the burial ground adjoining the meetinghouse. It is now known as Quaker House and used for First Day School, retreats, and workshops.

SOURCE: *Quakers in West Falmouth - 1685 to 1985*, a compilation of information from various publications, newspaper clippings, and local Friends.

Framingham Friends Meetinghouse

Framingham, Massachusetts
Erected: 1839
Location: Corner of Nixon and Edmands Roads
Burial Ground: No
In Use as Quaker Meetinghouse

The present meetinghouse was acquired in 1963 from the town of Framingham for one dollar. It is the former Schoolhouse Number Seven, built in 1839 at a total cost of approximately $1,100, under the supervision of a town committee consisting of Warren Nixon, Nathan Stone, and Abner Wheeler. Brothers Matthew and Alpheus Moulton were the builders. The building is oak post and beam construction, twenty-nine feet by thirty-eight feet, with ten-foot ceilings. It was vacant after 1915, and in 1926 the town authorized its sale by auction, but no action was taken. Neighbors maintained the building until Friends acquired the building and moved it about 150 feet to its present site and added a lower level. An addition in the form of a Sunday school room was added in 1974 at a cost of $33,000.

SOURCE: Paul Gardescu.

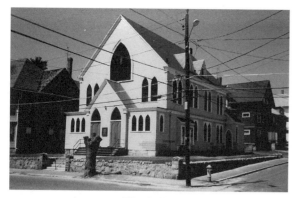

Lawrence Friends Meetinghouse

Lawrence, Massachusetts
Erected: 1895
Location: 45 Avon Street
Burial Ground: No
No Longer in Use as Quaker Meetinghouse

The meetinghouse in Lawrence has remained substantially unchanged since its construction. It stands on land donated by the Durant family to the Boston Monthly Meeting, under which Lawrence was a preparative meeting. When it became a monthly meeting in 1907, the land was transferred to it.

This building is an outstanding example of the southern New England Quaker architecture typical of the period when pastoral Friends were in the ascendancy. It is a church, not a meetinghouse. Gothic revival in style, it is similar to the Roxbury (Boston) Friends Church. It has stained glass windows, a pointed arch, wood trim, scissor trusses, and retains its original furnishings and lighting fixtures.

In the fall of 1985 the building and its contents were sold for the sum of $50,000 to the

Iglesia Christana Methodista Church of Lawrence with the stipulation that the property be used for religious purposes for the next twenty years.

SOURCE: Allan Sifferlen, Cambridge and Lawrence Immigrant Archives.

Acushnet Friends Meetinghouse

Long Plain (Acushnet), Massachusetts
Erected: 1735
Location: 1341 Main Street, near the intersection
  with Quaker Lane
Burial Ground: Yes
No Longer in Use as Quaker Meetinghouse
National Register of Historic Places; Museum

By 1735 Friends in the north part of Acushnet were so numerous that a two-story, thirty by forty-foot house with galleries was constructed for their use. It had chimneys and fireplaces, but there is no record of stoves.

A hundred years, later, additions included a vestibule, stoves, and horse sheds. In 1900 the inside of the building was remodeled and painted, and cushions and carpeting were added.

That same year the burial ground behind the meetinghouse was re-graded, leaving no stones visible.

By about 1965, the building was no longer used and in a sad state of disrepair. The "Friends of the Friends Meeting House," in cooperation with the Acushnet Historical Commission, organized to save the building, which was placed on the National Register of Historic Places. This meetinghouse is now a museum of Quaker artifacts and documents. It is open to the public on weekends, June through mid-September. The burial ground is now cared for by the town.

SOURCE: Information and materials supplied by Irwin Marks, Chairman of the Acushnet Historical Commission.

Lynn Friends Meetinghouse

Lynn, Massachusetts
Erected: 1816
Location: Sillsbee Street
Burial Ground: Adjacent to nearby modern
**   meetinghouse**
No Longer in Use as Quaker Meetinghouse

The first meetinghouse in Lynn was built in 1678 on Broad Street on a spot then known as Wolf Hill, a few rods east of Sillsbee Street near the Friends burial ground. It remained there until 1723. The second meetinghouse, on roughly the same site, measured forty feet long by thirty feet wide, with an extension on the east side used for women's business meeting. This building remained until 1816, when Thomas Rich purchased it and moved it westward to use as a warehouse. Five years later, James Breed bought it and moved it near his wharf at Broad and Beech Streets. The building's extension, sold separately to Nathan Alley, was moved to what was then Exchange Street opposite the Exchange Block, and used there as a dwelling. Later it was moved to Layette Street near Collins Street.

In 1816 the third meetinghouse was built on land given by Richard Estes. The building originally faced Broad Street, but in 1852 it was moved to face Sillsbee Street at the corner of Friends Street, and a basement was dug. This meetinghouse was sold in 1954, a year after Lynn Friends had moved to modern, spacious quarters at 20 Philips Street. Coming full circle, three years later Lynn Friends moved into another modern building on the site of the very first meetinghouse near Sillsbee Street. The original burial ground is in the rear of this building.

SOURCE: *Sketches* of *Lynn* by David N. Johnson, Greenwood Press, Westport, Connecticut, 1880. Additional information found in newspaper clippings from the Lynn Public Library archives.

Mattapoisett Friends Meetinghouse

Mattapoisett, Massachusetts
Erected: circa 1827
Location: On Route 6 in East Mattapoisett
Burial Ground: Yes
In Use as Quaker Meetinghouse

Major renovations of the interior walls, floors, benches, and other parts were completed in 1985, but no structural changes were made. A community house with indoor bathrooms replacing an outhouse, was built behind the meetinghouse in 1992.

SOURCE: Ruth Martocci.

Leverett, Massachusetts
(Mount Toby Friends Meeting)
Erected: 1963
Location: 194 Long Plain Road
    (on Route 63, north of Amherst town line)
Burial Ground: Yes
In Use As Quaker Meetinghouse

Members of Mt.Toby Meeting broke ground in 1993 for their meetinghouse at a meeting for worship in the field where it would be built. They had their first meeting for worship in the new building on 9th Month, 1964. The building stands on land given by Ethel Dubois, who had developed the rest of her farm into the Long Plain Nature Center. The Meeting acquired 112 acres of the farm in 1972, and has used it for agriculture (vegetable gardens, grain corn for overseas donation, sheep pastures and managed forest land) and outdoor recreation.

Architect Elroy Webber of Springfield drew from his visits to many old meetinghouses and specifications designated by meeting committees, for the design of the building. The worship room has a arched ceiling using laminated barn beams to çut the cost. Thirty wooden benches are formed in a hollow square with seating for one hundred. Other rooms included a library area, large fellowship room with fireplace, and folding walls to divide it; a small kitchen, office, nursery, and a multi-purpose room.

The cost of the original building was $80,000. A burial ground was established in 1985. The original electric heating system was replaced with oil hot water.

Mount Toby Friends Meetinghouse

The meetinghouse has been used for the Sanctuary program for two Central Americans. It also has been rented to a cooperative nursery school, and a public preschool for the Town of Leverett.

An addition was added in 1997, and the original rooms were redesigned to make a larger kitchen and to move the two-thousand-book library out of the entrance hall and into its own room, opening that hall to look out a flower garden. The addition was a room with large windows, which can be adapted to First Day School, discussion groups, singing at the piano, and showing videos or exhibiting pictures. The meeting room has an audio loop for the hearing impaired, which can broadcast to other rooms, and there is a accessible bathroom.

The meeting historian says these changes "have had a wonderful effect on the meeting because a new generation of Friends have planned and carried them out. "There is increased attendance—attenders now come from more than twenty-six towns—and new groups have been formed (painting, Bible study, singing, and environmental discussion). Mount Toby is one of the few meetinghouses in New England Yearly Meeting big enough for Young Friends weekends."

The meeting has also always done its own janitorial work, she says, and maintenance like painting the exterior, and shingling the roof "until we realized we had 70-year-old people working on the roof," and it was time to hire a professional.

SOURCES: John and Georgana Foster.

65

Nantucket Meetinghouse on Pine Street

Nantucket Meetinghouse on South Water Street

Nantucket, Massachusetts
Erected: 1701
Location: Pine Street
Private Residence

Nantucket was once largely Quaker. Due to divisions within the Society among Wilbur's, Gurney's, and Hicks' followers, there at one time existed four different meetinghouses. The first meetinghouse on Nantucket is believed to have been built in 1701 near Hummock Pond. In 1716, with increased membership, this building was lengthened by twenty feet. Again outgrown in 1820, the building was removed (in whole or in part) to its present location at 10 Pine Street. It was then incorporated by Quaker carpenter John Folger into a double dwelling, a two-and-a-half story, shingle structure on a brick foundation. It was later called Parliament House because of the meetings held in the "great room" of owner Friend Starbuck.

SOURCE: E.A. Stackpole, *Ramblings*, page 51; *Quakerism on Nantucket* by Burnham N. Dell, Nantucket Historical Society, 1970.

Nantucket, Massachusetts
Erected: Circa 1827
Location: South Water Street
Burial Ground: No
No Longer in Use as Quaker Meetinghouse

After the division of 1827 between Orthodox and Hicksite Friends, the Hicksite branch built their own meetinghouse on Main Street. Falling into disuse, it eventually became a hat factory and then a place of entertainment. Later it was moved to Brant Point, where it became part of the Nantucket Hotel. When the hotel closed in 1917, the structure was moved to its present site on South Water Street, where it was first called Red Men's Hall. Today it is the Dream Land Theater.

SOURCE: Burnham N. Dell, *Quakerism on Nantucket*, Nantucket Historical Society, 1970.

Nantucket Meetinghouse on Center Street (Gurneyite)

Nantucket Meetinghouse on Fair Street

Nantucket, Massachusetts
Erected: Circa 1846
Location: 29 Center Street
Burial Ground: No
No Longer in Use as Quaker Meetinghouse

After the division between the followers of Joseph John Gurney and John Wilbur among New England Friends in 1845, Gurneyite Friends built a meetinghouse at what is now 29 Center Street. A two-and-a-half-story Greek revival style clapboard building, it has a gable end facing the street, and shafts at the corners. This meeting, called "the larger body" because Gurneyites outnumbered the Wilburites, was laid down in 1867, and worship was discontinued in 1886. In 1894, according to archival records, the house was sold for use as a dwelling. Later it was used as a Baptist Church, and then as a dining hall for Bayberry Inn (today called Quaker House Inn).

SOURCE: E.A. Stackpole, *Ramblings*, page 18; Clay Lancaster, *Architecture of Nantucket*, page 166.

Erected: 1838
Location: 7 Fair Street
Burial Ground: No
In Use as Quaker Meetinghouse

The meetinghouse on Fair Street was first built as a school for the children of Friends who worshipped in a larger building next door. Later Friends sold their meetinghouse and moved into what had been their school. It was sold in 1864 when the meeting was discontinued. Additions were made to the structure. In 1894 the meetinghouse became the property of the Nantucket Historical Society, which presently maintains it. Since 1939 members of the Religious Society of Friends have been granted permission to use the old meetinghouse for worship according to the Quaker manner on Sunday mornings. The Nantucket Worship Group currently meets on Sunday mornings year-round in the meetinghouse.

SOURCES: Burnham N. Dell, *Quakerism on Nantucket*, Nantucket Historical Society, 1970; "Notes on the History of Quakerism on Nantucket," Nantucket Historical Society.

New Bedford Friends Meetinghouse

Newburyport Friends Meetinghouse

New Bedford, Massachusetts
Erected: 1822
Location: Corner of Spring and Seventh Streets
Burial Ground: No
In Use as Quaker Meetinghouse

New Bedford Meeting was established in the 1690s and became a monthly meeting in 1772. The present meetinghouse was erected on the site of the first one, which had been built in 1758 on land donated by Joseph Russell, although a marker on the building gives the date as 1715. The earlier building was later moved across the street, where it still stands.

SOURCE: *The New Bedford Standard Times*, 9th month, 8th, 1984.

Newburyport, Massachusetts
Erected: 1743
Location: Ferry Road, near Noble Street
Burial Ground: Yes
Private Residence

Amesbury Monthly Meeting granted permission for a Newbury meeting in 1714. The meetinghouse, a plain structure thirty feet by forty feet with two stories, was erected on the southwest side of High Street near the present Woodland Street, on a site conveyed by Stephen Sawyer for a Quaker burial ground. In 1825 a committee of Friends was authorized to sell the meetinghouse and "ground under and adjoining," and a quit-claim deed was given to Josiah Little. In that same year, the building became a private school run by Mrs. Upham, sister of a Bowdoin College professor. Later it became the vestry for the town's Fourth Parish Church. In 1857 it was moved to its present location on Ferry Road, not far from Noble Street, and is now a private residence.

SOURCE: *History of Newbury, Massachusetts, 1635 to 1902* by John J. Currier.

Northampton Friends New Meeting Room

Northampton, Massachusetts
Erected: Circa 1850, remodeled 2001
Location: 43 Center Street
Burial Ground: No
In Use as Quaker Meetinghouse

After ten years of meeting in quarters graciously provided by Smith College, Northampton Friends Meeting is looking forward to quarters in the center of Northampton.

The meeting is purchasing two portions, about 3,100 sq. ft. and 450 sq. ft., of the second floor of a building that is being renovated in the heart of Northampton. Architect Lynn Posner Rice has designed space for worship and classrooms that the children can feel are theirs. This downtown space gives the meeting a visible presence in the community. The monthly meeting minute of 2nd mo., 13th 2001 for approval of purchase of the property states: "There is unity in the belief that our individual and collective ministries both within the Meeting and within the community can be served best through purchase and right use of this space."

The building was constructed as a Methodist Church around 1880 and renovated by the Elks Club for their needs in 1912, and then again in 1924 and 1960. It is within a block of four other churches and right next door to the police station. Children will be able to play outdoors using the facilities of the neighboring People's Institute. The bus stops right around the corner, and the meeting will be in easy walking distance of Smith College.

The meeting intends to share use of the space with other groups to the fullest extent that does not hamper our own use. An interfaith emergency cot shelter will be located in the basement and there is the possibility of social service agencies in the building with which the meeting shares many interests.

The budget for the meetinghouse is $540,000. The meeting plans to be in its new space sometime between August and October, 2001.

Northampton Friends first met for worship 3rd mo., 17th 1991 on the Smith College campus. Northampton Friends Meeting was approved as a monthly meeting by Connecticut Quarterly Meeting on 2nd mo., 6th 1994.

Source: Bruce Hawkins, building committee.

Artist's sketch of Northampton Friends Center Street Property with meeting room on right.

Pembroke Friends Meetinghouse (restored)

Pembroke, Massachusetts
Erected: 1706
Location: Corner of Washington and
Schoosett Streets
Burial Ground: Yes
No Longer in Use as Quaker Meetinghouse
Massachusetts State Register of Historic Places

Pembroke was originally a preparative meeting under Sandwich Monthly Meeting. The site of this meetinghouse was donated by Robert Baker of Jamestown, Rhode Island, 6th month, 1st, 1709, although the building was believed to have been built three years earlier. The building, with its peaked roof, clapboard, and shingles, is of post and beam construction, and has a gallery that may be reached by climbing the narrow stairs on each side of the vestibule. The benches are handmade, and there is a woodshed and former privy attached to the northeast corner. Some alteration may have occurred in 1838, at which time the date of 1706 was found lettered-out in handmade nails on a door.

Pembroke Meetinghouse is on the Massachu-

setts State Register of Historic Places, and the history of its preservation is interesting. Abandoned by 1900, it was barely saved from being used for a Fourth of July bonfire in 1928 when Gilbert West, a descendant of Quakers, intervened and with the help of Horace T. Fogg of Norwell raised funds for its restoration. Later, meetings were held in the summer by Friends from Cambridge, Providence, and New Bedford, but the building gradually fell into disrepair until the Pembroke Historic District Commission acquired and restored the building in 1987. Detailed drawings made in the 1930s are available from the historic building survey.

A small graveyard on the half-acre plot has thirty-eight stones.

SOURCE: Numerous documents provided by Elizabeth Bates, Chairman, Pembroke Historic District Commission.

(Left) Pembroke Friends Meetinghouse, circa 1920s
(Below) Pembroke Friends Meetinghouse (1987) before restoration

Kevin J. Fachetti

East Sandwich Friends Meetinghouse

East Sandwich, Massachusetts
Erected: 1810
Location: Quaker Road
Burial Ground: Yes
In Use as Quaker Meetinghouse

East Sandwich Meeting is especially of interest historically—it is said to be the oldest Quaker meeting in America. It was founded in the winter of 1656-57 under the influence of Nicholas Upsall, a well-known Quaker minister. The meeting apparently did not have a regular meetinghouse for the first fifteen years, but according to the minutes of a meeting for business held on 4th month, 25th, 1672 construction of one was then underway. (They mention the thatching of the roof of Cape Cod's first meetinghouse.)

Construction of a second meetinghouse was begun on the present site in 1704, and the building was enlarged by Joseph Snow in 1709 and again in 1757 as the meeting grew. John Woolman, the famous New Jersey Quaker who worked tirelessly to persuade Quakers to disown slavery, attended meeting here on 7th month, 4th,

East Sandwich Friends burial ground (above), meeting room (left), entry (below)

Anthony I. Baker

71

1760. A story is told that Samuel Dottridge, a Quaker carpenter whose house in Scituate (now maintained by that town's historical society) dates back to 1790, would walk ten miles each way to attend East Sandwich Meeting every First Day.

The posts and beams of the frame of the present meetinghouse were actually cut on the Kennebec River in Maine and assembled on site. The third building on this site, it was dedicated on the 4th of July, 1810. The meetinghouse, a two-story structure which measures forty-eight by thirty-six feet, used to be called "The Great Meetinghouse" because it was such a large meetinghouse for its day. Though its balconies are now floored over, at one time the building could accommodate several hundred people.

Privies still stand back-to-back in a row along the building's north wall, and a carriage shed still stands as well. East Sandwich Friends have built a new, more modern structure for general use near the older meetinghouse.

In the large burial ground, the oldest stone bears the inscription, "Rose Jennings, died 1720." A large area nearby may be the site of earlier graves, unmarked in keeping with the then-prevalent custom of not using gravestones.

An old Quaker home, owned by the Wing family, is near this site. Open to the public, it houses a large collection of Quaker memorabilia.

East Sandwich Quarter is believed to be the third-oldest quarterly meeting in New England, dating from 1706.

SOURCE: *The Society of Friends on Cape Cod* by James Warren Gould, June 15, 1978.

EAST ELEVATION
SCALE 1/8" = 1'-0"

(North Elevation)

South Berkshire Friends Meetinghouse

Great Barrington, Massachusetts
Erected: circa 1985; remodeled 1999; addition 2001
Location: 280 Main Road
Burial Ground: No
In Use as Quaker Meetinghouse

South Berkshire Friends began meeting in the early 1950s with informal meditation and discussion at the home of Abbie and Raymond Olds in Monterey, Massachusetts, and then at Gould Farm, also in Monterey. By 1954, the group was an allowed meeting and had moved meetings to the home of Margaret and Lester Clark in South Lee where they met for the next twenty-eight years. The meeting was set off from Mount Toby Meeting as South Berkshire Monthly Meeting in 1984.

Increased numbers in the 1980s, in response to outreach by Storrs and Shirley Olds, led the meeting to larger quarters at Bard College and then to even larger rental space. A search committee formed in 1997 investigated more than one hundred building sites before the meeting bought thirty acres of meadow, mountainside, and swampland only half a mile from Great Barrington in 1999. Members remodeled an existing ranch house on the property until they could build on a large meeting room.

The search committee evolved into a construction committee, and after many meetings, the meeting found unity on a basic plan of construction for the meeting room. Members of the meeting helped raise funds, remodel, and build a parking lot. Construction on the new addition began in the spring of 2001.

Sources: David McAllester, Margaret Clarke, and Lester Clarke.

Sturbridge, Massachusetts (Bolton Friends Meetinghouse)

Sturbridge, Massachusetts
Erected: 1797
Location: Old Sturbridge Village, Sturbridge, MA
Burial Ground: No
No Longer in Use as Quaker Meetinghouse

Bolton meeting, a preparative meeting under Uxbridge Monthly Meeting, built this meetinghouse on the corner of Fry Road and Quaker Lane for a cost of $945.14. It measures thirty-four by twenty-eight feet and is two stories high. In 1818 it was enlarged by twenty feet and a dividing partition, shutters, and a woodshed were added. In 1872 two separate exterior entryways were built. These were later removed, though one was later added again.

Bolton Meeting was laid down in 1952, and in 1954 the building was given to Old Sturbridge Village, a living history museum, and moved to its new site there. It has now been restored to its original state, although the dividing partition has not been preserved.

SOURCE: Anne Humes.

William C. Janda

Bolton Friends Meetinghouse on original site before its restoration at Sturbridge Village. Photo: William Janda.

73

Swansea Friends Meetinghouse

Somerset (Swansea), Massachusetts
Erected: 1702
Location: 875 Prospect Street, Somerset
Burial Ground: Yes
In Use as Quaker Meetinghouse

Friends were among the early settlers in Swansea. It is recorded that on 1st month, 31st, 1702, money was collected to finish the Wickapimset Meetinghouse, as it was then called. It is believed that this earlier structure may be part of the present building, since there are records of enlargements made in 1746, 1872, and 1889. It has been renovated since then.

According to a history written in 1975, this meeting had twenty-one ministers, starting with Abraham Chase in 1727 and including Patience Brayton, an early and effective anti-slave worker, who served for twenty-one years. In the 1840s, during the split that divided the followers of John Wilbur and Joseph John Gurney, Thomas Wilbur, John's nephew, was clerk of Swansea Meeting. Wilbur refused to give up his position and turn over the meeting's records to the new clerk

appointed by New England Yearly Meeting, which had not been notified of any change in officers at Swansea for years. The records remained unsurrendered for the next twenty years, finally ending up in the vault of the Washington Street Trust Company in Westerly, Rhode Island, and then to the New England Yearly Meeting Archives in Providence.

The burial ground is at the rear of the present meetinghouse.

SOURCE: Information supplied by Janice W. Chace.

Uxbridge Friends Meetinghouse

Uxbridge, Massachusetts
Erected: 1770
Location: Highway 46 and the corner of
**   Aldrich Road**
Burial Ground: Yes
Occasional Use as Quaker Meetinghouse
Presently under the care of the Uxbridge
**   Quaker Meetinghouse Association**

In 1770 Smithfield Quarterly Meeting approved the construction of a meetinghouse in Uxbridge, and Moses Farum provided two parcels of land for a meetinghouse and cemetery for the price of six pounds. The two-story building, framed with local white oak, was completed 5th month 1771 at a cost of two hundred and six pounds, eight shillings, and one pence. The meetinghouse is thirty-five feet long by thirty feet wide, with a fireplace at the west end. The stone used in its construction came from nearby Good Stone Brook, and Friend Benjamin Taft forged the hardware and nails. The walls are fourteen inches thick and were made of brick kilned by Friend Ananias Gifford.

In 1850 the single, center door was replaced by two doors and an outside vestibule, and a fireplace was added in the east end. Moveable wooden partitions were installed to separate the men's and women's business meetings.

Uxbridge Friends Burying Ground

Regular meetings for worship were discontin-

ued in 1870. In 1910 the house and burial ground were placed under the care of Worcester Meeting, which held the property until the Meetinghouse Association took it over in 1952. The Association holds meetings, occasional weddings, and an annual ecumenical Thanksgiving service in the building. The horse sheds to the side of the building have been restored.

SOURCE: Anne Humes.

Wellesley Friends Meetinghouse (new addition)

Wellesley, Massachusetts
Erected: 1992 (addition)
Location: 26 Benvenue Street
Burial Ground: No
In Use as Quaker Meetinghouse

This meeting was allowed by Cambridge until it was formed as a monthly meeting in 1958. The present meetinghouse, which had earlier been a barn, was acquired in 1965 after Pine Manor Junior College, which had been using it as a dormitory, moved. Wellesley Friends Meeting used the "parlor" as a meeting room from 1965 to 1992.

The meeting completed the building of a new meetinghouse in April, 1992, next to the original building. The present meetinghouse includes a meeting room that has benches for about 130 people, an entry room, a coat room, and a rest room. The buildings were connected about three or four years later.

Westport (Central Village) Friends Meetinghouse

Wellesley Friends Meetinghouse (original)

Source: Finley Perry.

Westport (Central Village), Massachusetts
Erected: 1814
Location: 938 Main Road
Burial Ground: Yes
In Use as Quaker Meetinghouse

The first Westport meetinghouse was built on land acquired in 1716 for "three pounds current money" from George Cadman, which consisted of "one acre and a half and sixteen rods" about two miles north of Central Village. The building was twenty-eight feet wide and thirty-two feet long, with sixteen to seventeen-foot studs. Later, an ell on the east side was used for winter meetings. This building stood until 1813, when it was decided that a new and larger house was needed. The new building at the present site originally measured forty-five by thirty feet, with galleries, fireplaces, and a porch measuring fourteen feet by ten feet. Completed in 3rd month, 1814, costs came to two dollars less than the estimated $1,200.

This building was drastically remodeled in 1872. The major changes made at that time, including the removal of galleries and fireplaces, resulted in the house that stands today. One of the original features still extant is the women's horse block, with its eight-foot square granite top slab.

This meeting was the home meeting of a number of prominent Friends, including Paul Cuffe, a black merchant and sea captain famous for his anti-slavery efforts in the first part of the nineteenth century and a friend of First Lady Dolley Madison. More recently, Wilber K. Thomas and Clarence Pickett both served as executive secretaries of the American Friends Service Committee, and Edwin Hinshaw, a missionary to Kenya in the early 1960s.

There is a Friends burial ground adjacent to the present meetinghouse, and another at the site of the earlier meetinghouse.

SOURCE: Charles A. Brightman and Louise H. Tripp.

Worcester-Pleasant Street Friends Meetinghouse

Worcester, Massachusetts
First Erected: 1857
Second Erected: 1907-08
Third Erected: Mid to late 1800s
Location: 901 Pleasant Street (Third)
Burial Ground: No
In Use as Quaker Meetinghouse

In the early 1800s, Worcester Friends met informally over a store owned by a Friend, located at the corner of Main and Walnut Streets (known as the Paine Block).

In 1857 the first meetinghouse was built on the corner of Oxford and Division (now Shatham) Streets on a 120-foot square lot given by members Anthony Chase and Samuel H. Colton. The lot cost $1,500, and the building and horse shed in back of it $3,004.25.

In 1907 construction began on a larger brick and stone Friends church on the same site. The design was by Stephen Earle, a Friend and prominent Worcester architect, and the contractor was the G. H. Cutting Company. The cost was

$21,999. The new house was dedicated on 5th month, 10th, 1908, a snowy day. Eight thousand dollars of the funds came from the Timothy Earle Trust. One hundred dollars came from the sale of the Pomfret Meetinghouse in 1907. During construction, Friends sold a strip of land forty feet by one-hundred-and-twenty feet on the lot's northern side.

In 1946 an adjoining building was purchased for a parsonage, community center, and First Day School, but by 1971 membership had dwindled and the buildings could no longer be maintained. They were sold to the New School, which later sold the meetinghouse to a local repertory theater. The parsonage is now a two-family dwelling.

Through the efforts of the Worcester Heritage Preservation Society, the meetinghouse is on the National Register of Historic Sites, as a part of the Crown Hill Historic District.

In the 1970s the meeting purchased a Victorian home at 901 Pleasant Street, the current meetinghouse. One interior wall was removed to enlarge space for a meeting room. More recently, handicapped facilities have been added.

First Worcester Friends Meetinghouse

Second Worcester Friends Meetinghouse

SOURCE: Anne Humes and Betty Jones.

78

Yarmouth Friends Meetinghouse

South Yarmouth, Massachusetts
Erected: 1809
Location: 58 North Main Street
Burial Ground: Yes
In Use as Quaker Meetinghouse

It is believed that this meeting was started in 1681 as an allowed meeting under the care of Sandwich Monthly Meeting, and that it met in the homes of Friends named Dillingham and Jones until the first meetinghouse was erected in 1714 near the upper end of Bass River. The site of this building and a small adjacent burial ground may still be seen off Mayfair Road in what is now the town of Dennis. It is likely that this structure, or parts of it, were moved in the late 1700s to South Yarmouth, when that town was known as Quaker Village.

The present structure on North Main Street was built on land donated by David and Bathsheba Kelley, and may be a duplicate of the earlier meetinghouse. It is a substantial one-story frame building with a large entrance foyer and double doors. A clock built by Ezra Kelley (1798-1895) is mounted on a board from the old South Yarmouth salt works. The interior has the traditional moveable dividing shutters, but the women's side is larger than the men's side — possibly because so many of the men would often be away at sea. Some early whale oil lamps are still in place, and the traditional facing seats remain. Storms and age have claimed many of the large trees that lined North Main Street in the meetinghouse's earlier days.

An adjacent burial ground was laid out at the time of construction. In the southeast corner of the grounds stands a Quaker schoolhouse built in the 1820s which was moved from elsewhere in town to this site and is now is used for social events and First Day School.

The meeting at South Yarmouth was laid down in 1909, just one hundred years after the building was raised. It was re-established in 1954 on the same site and has prospered since then.

SOURCE: Barbara Ditmars, South Yarmouth, 1st month 1986, based on information by Laurence Barber, Donald Kelley and others.

Massachusetts Meetinghouses No Longer Standing

A. H. McCreary

Acushnet (Parting Ways) Friends Meetinghouse

Acushnet, Massachusetts

There are two burial grounds here, across the street from each other. The older of the two (closest to the former site of the meetinghouse) has only a few grave markers, but it is reported that it contains many more unmarked graves. Reports indicate that by about 1890 the stones in the cemetery were placed below ground and the entire area graded and grassed to create a small park.

SOURCE: *History of the Town of Acushnet* by Franklyn Howland (furnished by Irwin Marks, Acushnet Historical Society).

Assonet, Massachusetts

Built in 1727 in what was known as the Crystal Springs area of the village, the meetinghouse structure was moved to Friend and Main Street and replaced in 1896. It later became the dining hall of the Fall River Boys Camp until it was torn down and replaced by a regular dining hall in 1956.

The Fall River Camp was started by Thomas Chew, a deacon of the Congregational Church, and his wife for the poor children of Fall River. John Dean, a Quaker minister without descendants donated two farms, one on which the meetinghouse stood, for the camp.

Blackstone (South Mendon) Friends Meetinghouse

Blackstone (South Mendon), Massachusetts

Records indicate that a meetinghouse was built in 1812 near the north section of town on Elm Street, north of Handy Road and about two and a half miles south of the Mendon Friends Cemetery and Meetinghouse. There was a burying ground on the property.

SOURCE: Anne Humes.

Douglas, Massachusetts

Land was purchased in 1793 and a meeting-house erected that existed as late as Civil War times, when in a state of disrepair it was moved away and rebuilt as a shed. Town history states that "a small crude Quaker Meeting House and adjacent cemetery existed on the south side of the junction of Pine and Vine Streets." Gravestones marked with initials are still there, as are the private cemeteries of two prominent early Quaker families, Chase and Aldrich.

Local history reports that for some time many people believed that the old structure was haunted by spirits from the adjoining graves, and that as many as one hundred people would gather to watch dim forms flitting by the windows and to hear sepulchral conversations. It was later concluded that the apparitions were caused by light being reflected through the uneven glass in the old panes.

SOURCE: Anne Humes.

Fall River Friends Meetinghouse (11th month, 1st, 1894)

Fall River, Massachusetts

A large number of Friends came to the Swansea (Fall River, then Troy) area after the end of King Philip's War. A meeting was established in Swansea in 1732. In 1818 there was approval for a Fall River Meeting, which was first held in the Troy Dye House—a part of the Troy Manufacturing Company. This was on Troy Street, later called Mill Street. In 1822, with permission and support of the quarterly meeting, a meetinghouse was built on North Main Street. It was thirty-four by thirty-eight feet with twenty-foot posts, a feature that suggests it must have been two stories high. The final cost was $1,059.25. Membership increased rapidly, and it is reported that "fifty-six male heads of families attended regularly." A new meeting was opened on the same site on the 12th day of the 12th month, 1836. The first structure was removed to the south side of Cherry Street and converted to a dwelling.

In 1844 a Wilburite group withdrew and met in a house at the corner of Franklin and High Streets. The building was known as the Green

Schoolhouse because the property had been purchased from school district number two. It was a two-story structure, built on rock without a foundation. First month, 12th, 1846, it was conveyed to Oliver Chase and Israel Buffinton. In 1861 there were seventy members but no minister. In 1872 the meeting was laid down and the lot sold. The meetinghouse pictured was sold in 1944 to the YMCA. It is now gone.

The iron gate is the entrance through a stone wall that surrounds the front part of a Friends burying ground at the corner of North Main and Hood Streets. There are fifteen identifiable stones. This is the burying ground for the former Hood Street Meeting, which was a preparative meeting under the care of Swansea Monthly Meeting. The site of the meetinghouse is now a parking lot.

SOURCE: Jeannette Denning; the Fall River Historical Society.

Leichester, Massachusetts

The first meetinghouse in 1739 was a one-story, twenty by twenty-two-foot building on land owned by Friend Robert Earle. A second and larger house was erected on the same site in 1891, the original building having been removed to become a private residence in Rutland. The second structure was a two-story building with galleries around three sides. It is not recorded when the building disappeared, but the meeting itself was laid down in 1855. Presently, four stone posts mark its site in the middle portion of the still functioning Leichester Friends Cemetery off Route 56 in Leichester. This four-acre tract, under the care of Worcester Monthly Meeting, is main-

tained with trust funds that include a $2,000 grant given by Robert Earle in 1887 in his will.

SOURCE: Anne Humes.

Mendon, Massachusetts

Between 1729 and 1850 a meetinghouse was apparently located next to the burying ground on the south side of George Road between North Avenue and Providence Street. Its parts were used to build a railroad station at Northbridge on the Providence and Worcester Railroad after it was taken down.

SOURCE: Anne Humes.

Nantucket, Massachusetts

A second meetinghouse was erected in 1722-33 at the corner of Main Street and Saratoga Street (now Quaker Road). A large burial ground, now under the care of the town, was also established. Several thousand Friends are buried there in unmarked graves, as was the early custom. The meetinghouse, thought to be too far from the center of town, was later removed to the northwest corner of Main and Pleasant Streets, where it was enlarged to a two story structure fifty-six feet long by thirty-eight feet wide.

When one of the divisions in the Society occurred, a small group split off and met in a small house on the site of the present Jarad Coffin Inn. The large meetinghouse on Main Street was later abandoned and became a warehouse on what was then Commercial Wharf. According to reports, the building burned down.

Newtown, Massachusetts

The Newtown Meetinghouse was built in 1754 in Smith Mills near the North Dartmouth Meetinghouse on a lot presented by Josiah Merrihew at an estimated cost of a thousand pounds in Rhode Island currency, with an initial subscription of 401 pounds. Later reports mention the location as Faunce Corner Road. In 1827, Dartmouth Meeting minutes record the building's being in serious disrepair and the meeting took up a subscription to restore it. The restoration was apparently accomplished in 1829, with a final settlement of cost in 1834. Another report names it as a new building in 1829 and lasting for sixty years when it was closed and memberships transferred to North Dartmouth. There is no report of what happened to the structure.

SOURCES: Souvenir of The Dartmouth Monthly Meeting published by Franklin Howland, 1899. Minutes of Dartmouth Monthly Meeting (1827) and Dartmouth *Chronicle*, May 14, 1970. Amy Lappin, New England Yearly Meeting Archives and George T. Berish of Dartmouth.

"The watering trough in front of the Northbridge Quaker Meetinghouse."

Northbridge, Massachusetts—torn down "The Second Quaker Meeting House, built in 1804. It was located next to present Quaker Cemetery."

Northbridge, Massachusetts

Land was purchased in 1773 and again in 1817. The meetinghouse and burying ground, which have been turned over to the town, were located in the eastern section of town on Quaker Street at Plummer Road, near the Blackstone River. The meetinghouse fell into decay and disappeared by 1912.

SOURCE: Anne Humes.

Pelham, Massachusetts

The first Friend in Pelham was Eseck Cook, who arrived in 1806. In 1808 Richmond Monthly Meeting purchased four acres of land from Samuel Arnold in the westerly part of town on "the highway leading from Amherst to Boston." On this property, a small plain one-story building was erected. At one point, in 1821, the Richmond overseers of the Pelham Preparative Meeting "removed its preparative status for having difficulty for keeping this meeting in the authority of the truth." The meeting gradually declined, and on 4th month, 4th, 1855, Uxbridge Monthly Meeting sold the property to Zeba Cook for $86.50. The building was later used as a barn and was still standing as late as 1898. A board from this structure was incorporated into Mount Toby Meetinghouse when it was built in 1963.

When the deed was conveyed to Cook, it contained a clause reserving forever the right of passage to a small cemetery of one quarter acre at the rear of the lot, and stipulated that "said graveyard is to be retained for use of said Society and is not intended to be conveyed by this deed."

A search of the land records indicates that after several transactions, this clause was omitted. The property is now in the hands of the town of Amherst, having been conveyed to them by the Amherst waterworks. There is a small burying ground on the property.

SOURCE: Joseph Larson, Pelham Cemetery Commission and *History of the Town of Pelham* by C.O. Parmenter, Amherst, Massachusetts, 1898.

Salem, Massachusetts

The first meetings in Salem were held in 1657 in private homes. Thomas Maule built the first

Salem Friends Meetinghouse (Second)

meetinghouse in 1688 and deeded it to Friends in 1690. It it estimated to have been twenty-five feet ten inches in length but somewhat less than that in width. The house was used for meetings until 1718, when it was deeded back to Thomas Maule. He added some rooms and converted it to a residence. It stood on Essex Street—approximately opposite the present city library—between 375 Essex and Grace Church.

The frame of a small red structure at the rear of the Essex Institute may be the original frame of this first meetinghouse, though another speculation is that it is from the First Congregational Meetinghouse.

The second Friends meetinghouse in Salem was erected in 1719 and stood at or near the Friends cemetery at 395 Essex. A residence at that corner bears a plaque inscribed "Quaker Meeting House." The original structure was forty feet by thirty feet and two stories high, but it is reported to have been torn down in 1832. Quaker archive records claim it was remodeled in 1903 and that it burned in 1914. Salem historical records report that Friends in 1832 built a brick meetinghouse on either Pine or Warren Streets (this may be the one that burned). There is a Friends burial ground on Charter Street.

Thomas Maule did more for Friends than build a meetinghouse. In 1694 he published *Truth Held Forth and Maintained*, in which he explained and defended Quaker views. At that time Quakers were considered as much of a threat as witches. The governor and council directed Salem's sheriff to search Maule's house and burn all copies of the offending work, and Maule was arrested for publishing a book "wherein is contained divers slanders against churches and the government of this Province."

SOURCE: Salem Public Library reference room and myself on foot.

Taunton, Massachusetts (cemetery only)

An atlas published in 1871 designates a site that corresponds to "The North West part of town," where the Taunton Meetinghouse was probably located. Both an earlier and a more recent map in the Taunton Public Library show a "Quaker Cemetery" near the corner of South Crane Avenue and Harvey Street on the southeast side, and it seems likely that the meetinghouse would have been located nearby.

SOURCE: Materials furnished by Darrell A. Ashcroft, Taunton Public Library.

West Newbury Friends Meetinghouse

West Newbury, Massachusetts

In 1744 Friends erected a meetinghouse on Turkey Hill on land conveyed to Seabrook Monthly Meeting by Robert Brown on 3rd month, 4th, 1829, with the stipulation that they "shall improve it for a Meeting House and hold a meeting for the worship of God." The house was rebuilt in 1882. Local resident Wallace Ordway bought it in 1917 , intending to move it, but this was not feasible because of the wartime man- power shortage, it was torn down two years later. Some of the timbers were used to add a sun porch to Ordway's home on Main Street.

In Fifth month, 21st, 1855, Josiah Little of Newburyport sold about one acre of land "on the road leading from Newburyport to West Newbury by Turkey Hill" to West Newbury Friends for a burying ground. Forty-two graves were at one time counted in this cemetery, though it has been neglected in recent years.

SOURCE: *Currier's History of Newbury*; E. R. Spencer Ordway of West Newbury provided a photo of the meeting- house taken in 1909.

Quaker Burial Grounds in Massachusetts

Adams, Massachusetts—

Near meetinghouse on Friends Street.

Acushnet, Massachusetts—

See Long Plain, Massachusetts.

Amesbury, Massachusetts—

Near meetinghouse at the corner of Friends and Greenleaf Streets. John Greenleaf Whittier and some of his family are buried there. Now a part of the town cemetery.

Apponegansett, Massachusetts—

Adjacent to meetinghouse on Russell's Mill Road. First laid out in 1706; enlarged in 1753.

Blackstone, Massachusetts—

See South Mendon, Massachusetts.

Douglas, Massachusetts—

1) South side of junction of Pine and Vine Streets; gravestones marked with initials;

2) Private cemeteries of Chase and Aldrich families on same site.

East Sandwich, Massachusetts—

Near meetinghouse; large area nearby may contain unmarked graves; oldest stone marked 1720.

Fall River, Massachusetts—

Corner of North Main and Hood Streets.

Leichester, Massachusetts—

Leichester Friends Cemetery on Route 56 in Leichester at the site of a former meetinghouse, marked by four posts in center of cemetery. The cemetery consists of four acres under care of Worcester Monthly Meeting. It is known locally as "spider gates" cemetery for the spider-like iron work on its gates.

Long Plain (Acushnet), Massachusetts—

Two, across the street from each other at the site of the meetinghouse; regraded in 1900, stones no longer visible. Under the care of the town.

Lynn, Massachusetts—

Behind current meetinghouse on Sillsbee Street.

Mattapoisett, Massachusetts—

Near meetinghouse on Route 6 in East Mattapoisett.

Mendon, Massachusetts—

Next to site of meetinghouse, south side of George Road between North Avenue and Providence Street.

Nantucket, Massachusetts—

Corner of Main Street and Quaker Road near site of second Nantucket meetinghouse, which was moved later; unmarked graves now under care of town.

Newbury, Massachusetts—

On road from Newburyport to West Newbury, near Turkey Hill.

Newburyport, Massachusetts—

Near Woodland Street, at original site of meetinghouse.

North Dartmouth, Massachusetts—

1) Chace Road; 2) Tucker Road.

Northbridge, Massachusetts—

Near sight of meetinghouse on Quaker Street at Plummer Road. Under the care of the town.

Pelham, Massachusetts—

In woods near Amherst Waterworks.

Pembroke, Massachusetts—

Near meetinghouse at the corner of Washington and Schoosett Streets.

Salem, Massachusetts—

Friends Cemetery at 395 Essex Street.

Somerset, Massachusetts—

At rear of meetinghouse, 875 Prospect Street.

South Mendon (Blackstone), Massachusetts—

1) Mendon Friends Cemetery;

2) At site of meetinghouse on Elm Street north of Handy Road; laid out in 1812.

South Yarmouth, Massachusetts—

1) Off Mayfair Road in what is now the town of Dennis at the site of the first South Yarmouth meetinghouse;

2) Adjacent to present meetinghouse at 58 North Main Street. Laid out in 1809.

Swansea, Massachusetts—

See Somerset, Massachusetts.

Taunton, Massachusetts—

Corner of South Crane Avenue and Harvey Streets, on southeast side.

Uxbridge, Massachusetts—

Near meetinghouse at Highway 46 and Aldrich Road.

West Falmouth, Massachusetts—

Adjacent to meetinghouse. Take Route 28 south from Bourne Bridge to Thomas Landers Road; go south on Route 28A, 1 1/2 miles to meetinghouse on right.

West Newbury, Massachusetts—

On the road leading from Newburyport to West Newbury by Turkey Hill.

Westport, Massachusetts—

1) Near present meetinghouse, 938 Main Road; 2) At site of earlier meetinghouse about two miles north of Central Village.

New Hampshire

New Hampshire

This is a special state for me because both my monthly and quarterly meetings are in New Hampshire, and also because I spent much of my working life traveling the state for the University of New Hampshire Cooperative Extension Service.

Most meetinghouses presently in use in the state are all at least a hundred years old and are essentially in their original architectural condition. The two exceptions are the meetinghouses in Hanover and Monadnock, which are recently acquired, converted dwellings. By type, the older buildings represent both the programmed and unprogrammed form of worship. Several former meetinghouses have either been converted to other uses or have disappeared entirely, although their site is still known. In some instances, as in the case of Newton, I was only able to locate a graveyard. Ruth Bragg of the local library says there is no record of there ever having been a meetinghouse.

A meetinghouse was built in Concord, the state capital, in 1815. This came about because a builder named Greely Hannaford from Portland, Maine happened into a Quaker meeting where a woman rose and spoke, according to his account, "so appropriately to my state of mind that I was astonished and like Paul, struck down to the ground at noontime." Following this transformative experience Mr. Hannaford became a Friend, and when his sister, Ruth, who ran a tavern in Concord, came to visit him he convinced her to become a Friend. Upon her return home, she started the first Friends meeting in Concord (1805), and in 1815 a meetinghouse was built on ground now occupied by the state capitol building. Levi Hutchins, a clockmaker, traveled to Weare Meetinghouse to make copies of the benches there, so that there would be uniformity among the meetinghouses in the area. In 1816, the building was moved to a lot on State Street. When the meeting was laid down in 1840, the house was sold to become a school. In 1859 it was moved to Franklin Street where it is presently a two-family home. The burying ground is marked by a memorial marker in the Old North Cemetery on State Street.

Unity Meetinghouse at Quaker City, with its plain and simple lines that have remained unchanged since it was built in 1820, is one of my favorite structures. Henry Osborne, in a note to me, reported that one farmer was too busy to leave a day early to attend a special meeting at Unity and sent his wife and children ahead in their horse and wagon. Later his conscience troubled him and he found a neighbor to do his chores and set out on foot to walk the forty miles, arriving the next day in time to join his family at worship. Henry wondered if there was anyone today who would do this.

Especially gratifying has been the devotion of a few young people in the area who have tended the building and adjoining shed of the Unity meeting house with loving care, replacing sills, roofs, and clapboards. Special thanks goes to Jennifer Wright and David Sawyer, as well as to the others who gathered for special work days arranged with the help of David Curtis and Donald Baker of Weare Meeting, under whose care the building was. I have in my file a whole set of letters and other materials, especially from Jenny Wright, which detail the long and difficult process of building rehabilitation.

Quaker City Friends had attended meeting at Weare until 1818, when permission was granted for a separate meeting; the members at Weare assisted in its construction.

Weare was the site of two early meetinghouses—North Meeting and South Meeting. About 1766, two Friends, Jonathan Dow and Elijah Purington, came to town and another fifty Quaker families followed. An early house was built in Weare Center near the present town hall. By 1795, the membership had become so large that two new meetinghouses were built. About the same time, a Friends burying ground was laid out on one acre at Center Square, presumably where the first meeting house had been. The town history notes that there were 567 members in 1820 and fewer than 200 by 1872. The decline was in part caused by the disownment of members who married outside of the Society. The history goes on to say that no Friends ever required help by the town because they were paupers, and none was ever arrested; they had few lawsuits, their animals were never impounded, and they never tolerated drunkards; they made their influence felt by their individual efforts to live the spirit of their religion. In 1920, with the meeting closed, the remaining Weare Friends united with the Congregationalists to form the Federated Church. This arrangement was ended in 1994.

The first recorded marriage among Friends in what was then Hampton (now Seabrook) took place at a special meeting held in 1705 at the house of Thomas Bernard, where John Peaslee and Mary Martin married. Forty-seven witnesses signed their marriage record.

In the town history of Richmond, which records a lawsuit over the placement and removal of gravestones from the Friends cemetery, it is noted that the meeting was not especially blessed with members gifted in ministry. A comment was included about Israel Saben "whose ministrations were favorably received by all who had the privilege of listening to his pathetic appeals." I assume the writer meant prophetic and not pathetic (at least I hope so).

A note in the Wolfeboro town history records the style of bonnets worn by Quaker women: "They were regulated by the age of the wearer which was changeless; the aged women wearing odd shaped black silk, middle aged white silk of the same shape, and young misses white silk with the front slightly flaring."

The present West Epping Meeting under the care of Gonic Monthly Meeting originally grew out of the Salem Quarter in the mid-1700s. Records show Joshua Fulsom as a recorded minister there in 1772. In the 1950s a Fulsom was still a recorded minister there.

I have a large volume of correspondence concerning Gilmanton Meeting and its associated burying ground. It turned out unexpectedly that title to the cemetery was held by Dover Monthly Meeting. After a great amount of diligent record searching by H.L. Osler, a Friend who had moved to Gilmanton and was on the town trust and cemetery committee, ownership was transferred to Gilmanton, which for years had had it under their care. It now has a marker as a Friends site.

Gilmanton is an interesting example of what happens to the property of laid-down meetings. A Mrs. Charles Taylor acquired some of the pews and used them as benches in her summer home. Other pews, some blinds, the pulpit, and most of the granite foundation stones were purchased by Mrs. William Scriven who turned the barn of the parents' summer home into a large recreation room, with the pews used as benches and the blinds as background screens. The old foundation stones were set around the brick terrace.

The Pittsfield *Town History* made this observation about Friends: "Hard work, clean living and good neighborliness were outward signs of a good Quaker and Pittsfield had its share of the best."

Regarding Dover Meeting, I haven't yet discovered what happened in the 1800s to cause its decline and subsequent laying down in the 1940s. Shirley Leslie, birthright member of Gonic Monthly Meeting, has promised to help me find the answer. Someplace in the present meeting house is a time capsule established when Dover completed its renovation in 1991 by raising the house and putting a basement under it to accommodate the growing First Day School. This is supposed to be opened in 100 years, but perhaps 2093, when the building will be 325 years old, would be a better date. It is the oldest house of religion in Dover and one of its oldest structures. A photograph printed in *Foster's Daily Democrat* in May 1910 shows a schoolhouse adjacent to the meetinghouse, near the present entrance road to Pine Hill Cemetery.

Meaderboro Friend, resident, and famous plant breeder, Elwin Meader was kind enough to furnish me with copies of minutes about the laying down and disposal of the New Durham and Gilmanton buildings. He thinks some of the boards from the Gilmanton structure may have been used to make repairs at the Meaderboro Meetinghouse (now a local church) to which a Sunday school annex was added in 1963. At that time, the old horse sheds were torn down to make way for the addition.

Lee in Four Centuries, the town of Lee's bicentennial booklet, contains valuable information about the former meetinghouse and Walnut Grove School that was once housed in it, as well as about the Cartland family who ran the school and were very active in the anti-slavery movement. Their home, which is still standing, was a way station on the underground railroad. One of the slaves who passed through there, Oliver Gilbert, returned in 1902 to farm with his son; it is said that he helped build the stone wall in front of the Cartland residence.

New Hampshire Meetinghouses

Concord Friends Meetinghouse

Concord, New Hampshire
Erected: 1815
Location: Franklin Street
Burial Ground: Yes, on separate site
Private Residence

In the early 1800s a builder named Greely Hannaford from Portland, Maine happened to attend a Quaker meeting one First Day. A woman rose and spoke, according to his account, "so appropriately to my state of mind that I was astonished and like Paul, struck down to the ground at noontime." Following this transformative experience Mr. Hannaford became a Friend, and when his sister Ruth, who owned a tavern in Concord, came to visit him he convinced her to become one, too. Upon her return home, she started the first Friends Meeting in Concord in 1805, and ten years later a meetinghouse was built approximately on the site of the present-day State House. In 1816, when the state of New Hampshire purchased the lot, the meetinghouse was moved to a location on State Street.

The meeting was laid down in 1840, and in 1845 the meetinghouse was sold and became a schoolhouse. In 1859 the building was again moved and later rebuilt as a residential duplex on Franklin Street, where it is still a private home today.

There is a small Friends burial ground with a memorial marker set aside in Concord's Old North Cemetery on State Street.

SOURCE: Charles Day

Dover Friends Meetinghouse

Dover, New Hampshire
Erected: 1768
Location: 141 Central Avenue
Burial Ground: No
In Use as Quaker Meetinghouse; National
   Register of Historic Buildings

The first Dover meetinghouse was reported to have been built about 1680 on Dover Neck. The second was erected in 1712 on land belonging to Ebenezer Varney. The deed, transferred to Friends in 1735, described the site as being "on the southeasterly side of the road which leads from Cocheco to Tolend near the place where Thomas Down's house stood—seventy by forty-foot lot bounded by Watson land." This location is believed to be the present corner of Locust and Silver Streets.

The third and present Dover meetinghouse is a large two-story building. It was built on land owned by Aaron Hanson and was raised 6th month, 9th, 1768 on a site larger than the present lot. This meetinghouse was the largest hall in

Dover for a number of years, and several public documents were reportedly read there at the time of the American Revolution. About 1800, a stove from Russia was installed and partly paid for from the sale of pine lumber from a four-acre lot across the street, which had been acquired in 1774 and used to pasture Friends' horses during meeting. The parents of John Greenleaf Whittier, the famous Quaker poet, were married in this meetinghouse in 1804.

A Dover city map of 1906 shows that there was once a large outhouse to the right rear of the meetinghouse. Though some remodeling has been redone in recent years to accommodate the needs of more modern Friends, the basic structure remains largely unchanged.

SOURCE: *History of Dover Friends Meeting* by Annie E. Pinkham. Also, Elwyn Meader of Meaderboro.

Designer's sketch of proposed renovations (2001)

Present Hanover Friends meeting room addition

Hanover, New Hampshire
Erected: Circa 1920-1930
Location: 43 Lebanon Street
Burial Ground: No
In Use as Quaker Meetinghouse

Many early New Hampshire Quaker meetings had their roots in farming communities, but Hanover is one of the exceptions. It exemplifies the newer meetings successfully established near major universities—in this case, Dartmouth College—that have occurred since World War II.

The first meetinghouse, on Rope Ferry Road, was a fine turn-of-the-century home originally built as a residence for the president of Dartmouth College. It was re-acquired by the college in a swap with the meeting. At the time of the exchange, Hanover Friends Meeting obtained its present meetinghouse at 43 Lebanon Street, a former residence that has since undergone substantial alteration, including the addition of a meeting room.

SOURCE: Pete Stettenheim and Treat Arnold.

Hanover Friends Meetinghouse from mid 1966 to 1984

Henniker Friends Meetinghouse

Lee Friends Meetinghouse

Henniker, New Hampshire
Erected: 1790
**Location: On Quaker Street, 3 miles south of
    village**
Burial Ground: Yes
In Use as Quaker Meetinghouse (except winters)

This meetinghouse remains essentially
unchanged—a long, low, single story structure of
post and beam construction with white, painted
clapboards. At one time the right side was a
dwelling with three rooms, but the partitions have
since been removed.

The interior is very plain, with simple
wooden benches. The center beam in the meeting
room is supported by a small-barked hemlock
post taken from a nearby beaver pond.

There is a burial ground about two hundred
yards east of the meetinghouse, next to an old
school that was known as Quaker School and
used until about 1950.

This meeting was laid down in 1940 and
reopened in 1973. It is under the care of Weare
Monthly Meeting and is closed in winter.

SOURCE: Donald Baker, Hillsboro, New Hampshire.

Lee, New Hampshire
Erected: Circa 1774
Location: North River Road
Burial Ground: Yes
Private Residence

This building is little changed from the time
when it was moved from a nearby but unknown
site to its present location opposite the old
Cartland residence. The building measures forty-
six by twenty-five feet, including the porch, and
has an attic containing two small rooms and one
large room.

Cartland Family Cemetery (Lee, New Hampshire)

Moses Cartland (1805-1863), who was a teacher at Moses Brown Friends School in Providence Rhode Island and at Friends' Seminary in Weare, later established Walnut Grove School in this meetinghouse. He taught here from 1847 to 1853 and again from 1860 to 1963, and the building's large open room still contains a raised platform. Cartland was a good friend of Quaker poet John Greenleaf Whittier. The Cartland home, which stands across the street, was a station on the Underground Railroad. Oliver Gilbert, a slave who passed through there to freedom, returned with his son to farm on the land in 1902. It is said that he helped to build the stone wall in front of the house.

The first meetinghouse in Meaderboro was built about 1796 near the present Rochester-Farmington town line and later moved to a site on the Vickery Farm.

The second meetinghouse was built to house a pastoral meeting on land conveyed for that purpose by Moses Jenness to Dover Monthly Meeting. Carriage sheds originally stood behind the building. Though in 1962 an annex containing a kitchen and Sunday school rooms was added, Meaderboro Meeting itself was laid down the next year, and the building transferred to the Meaderboro Community Church.

A large burial ground across the street is under the care of Gonic Monthly Meeting.

SOURCE and PHOTOS: Elwyn Meader

Meaderboro Friends Meetinghouse

Meaderboro (Rochester), New Hampshire
Erected: Circa 1872
Location: 151 Meaderboro Road
Burial Ground: Yes
No Longer in Use as Quaker Meetinghouse

Monadnock Friends Meetinghouse

Monadnock, New Hampshire
Erected: 1989
Location: On Route 202 from the South, 3 miles
    beyond Jaffrey
Burial Ground: No
In Use as Quaker Meetinghouse

A search for land on which to build was initiated in 1990. In January 1991 an option was taken on a piece of land, but later site problems cause the meeting to reject it and to consider existing buildings. In November of 1991 Bruce MacDougal, reporting for the site committee, recommended the purchase of a three-bedroom ranch house of 2,497 square feet, built in 1989 and owned by Marie Baird. The house was set on 5.7 acres of land on Route 202, at the juncture of the town lines of Jaffrey and Peterborough.

The meeting met the purchase price of $157,450 through a membership appeal, a loan request to the Peterborough Savings Bank, and appeals to various Friends organizations. The meeting eventually approved borrowing up to $100,000 from the Friends Extension Corporation. The Chace Fund contributed a $5,000 grant.

An interim building committee (Travis Belcher, Bruce MacDougal, Phyllis Stine Schultz and David Erikson) oversaw changes to the interior of the building to meet required codes set by the Jaffrey Planning Board. Initial approval was granted for a maximum capacity of forty-nine people. Later interior adjustments increased the size of the meeting room's the capacity to 120. A two-car garage was converted for classroom space.

The first meeting held in the house was on the first day of spring, March 22, 1992. At a later date, Helen Bliss gave a dedication talk at an open house attended by about a hundred people.

SOURCE: Silas Weeks, based on information found in three years of meeting minutes and notes from Virginia Towle; Ruth Herman, clerk.

Richmond Meetinghouse (now a private dwelling)

Richmond, New Hampshire
Erected: 1790
Burial Ground: Yes
Private Residence

Friends from Rhode Island were among the first settlers in Richmond, New Hampshire. The earliest meetings were held in the homes of Daniel Cass and Jedediah Buffum, under the care of Uxbridge (Massachusetts) Quarterly Meeting in 5th month 1766.

Richmond meetinghouse was built at Four Corners on four acres of land given to Friends by Jedediah Buffum. The property included land for a burial ground that is now maintained by the local historical society. A wood shed and covered horse stalls also stood near the meetinghouse.

The meeting prospered, becoming an independent monthly meeting in 1791, but by 1810 rigid regulations concerning birthright membership, marriage outside of the meeting, and other controversial matters caused a decline in membership. Among the factors that hastened the meeting's demise was a controversy that erupted around the year 1824 over gravestones. The meeting as a whole, consistent with early Quaker belief, considered marked graves to be a needless extravagance and refused to allow them. When, in defiance of the meeting's wishes, a Friend named Mowery Sabin marked the graves of his parents with plain marble slabs, the markers were removed at night and buried in the woods. A bitter lawsuit followed, but the court eventually ruled in favor of the meeting. Finally, in 1857, the meeting was laid down.

SOURCE: *History of the Town of Richmond.*

Gonic Friends Meetinghouse

Rochester, New Hampshire (Gonic Friends Meeting)
Erected: 1890
Location: 41 Pickering Road, Rochester
Burial Ground: Yes, at site of a different meeting
In Use as Quaker Meetinghouse

The Gonic Friends Meeting began with worship held in Friends' homes in 1743. In 1781 Friends received permission to build their first meetinghouse on the southeast corner of land belonging to Jonathan Dame on the road to Cocheco (now Dover), though there may have been problems since it wasn't until fourteen years later that the two-story, thirty by thirty-foot structure was finally built. Monthly meeting records report that about forty years later the Gonic Friends meetinghouse was in need of repairs and Friends again met in members' homes.

In 1847 this meetinghouse was dismantled and rebuilt near what is now the corner of Tibetts and Pickering Roads. It was then a one-story building and became known as the Pine Grove Meetinghouse. A year later, the Cocheco Railroad paid $133 for permission to run their tracks through the property. In 1862 the monthly meeting agreed with the members of Pine Grove Meeting to move the meetinghouse to a lot belonging to John Estes opposite the home of Mary Osborne. It was moved by oxen as a five-year-old boy named Fremont Jenness ran along by their side. The deed for the lot was recorded in 1870. Although the exact date is unknown, the Pine Grove meetinghouse was at some point moved down the right side of Mill Street and used to store lumber. An 1887 map shows both first and second meetinghouses.

The second and present meetinghouse was built by the Whipple brothers, who at that time managed the sawmill at the end of Mill Street. It is a single-story Greek revival style white clapboard structure with the gable end facing the street. A letter dated 1903 mentions a back room that was probably added to the present meetinghouse in 1902, perhaps to provide a convenient place to eat dinner when quarterly meeting was held. The Whipples also fashioned the unusual pews of natural golden oak that matched the interior woodwork.

There is an associated burial ground in Meaderboro, also a part of Rochester, across from the former Meaderboro Friends Meetinghouse. A small cemetery on Sixth Street in Dover, once used by the Meader family, is under the care of Gonic Friends.

SOURCE: Shirley Leslie, clerk of Gonic Friends Meeting.

Center Sandwich, New Hampshire
Erected: Circa 1862
Location: Maple Road
Burial Ground: Yes
Not in Use as Quaker Meeting

Sandwich Friends became a monthly meeting under Salem (Massachusetts) Quarterly Meeting in 1783. An early building, probably dating 1790, was purchased and moved to Tamworth, where it became known as the "Bean" meeting, because a Rev. David Bean, a Free Will Baptist minister lived next door to the meetinghouse. This building burned in 1849.

A second meetinghouse was built in Center Sandwich sometime between 1812 and 1816. This building is said to have cost $905 and to have been a two-story structure measuring thirty by fifty feet. It was burned in 1862 in the draft riots, when there were bitter feelings against Quakers because they refused to go to war.

A third building was then erected on land purchased by Ezra Gould from Timothy Varney. However, when membership declined in the early 1890s, the building was purchased and remodeled by the Sandwich Grange.

A well-tended burying ground under the care of the present town of Center Sandwich and North Sandwich Meeting may be found near Wentworth Hill in Center Sandwich.

Center Sandwich Friends Meetinghouse (1862)

SOURCE: Evelyn S. Wallace of Tamworth, and from a town history.

North Sandwich Friends Meetinghouse (original)

North Sandwich, New Hampshire
Erected: 1881
Location: 354 Quaker-Whiteface Road
Burial Ground: Yes
In Use as Quaker Meetinghouse
National Registry of Historic Buildings

The first meetinghouse in North Sandwich, built in 1814, stood a short distance northwest of the present building. When it fell into disrepair it was sold for $21; it may now be part of a shed or garage attached to the Schmidt house on Brown Hill.

William Quimby built the present meetinghouse in 1881 at a cost of approximately $1,000. In 1900, Friends purchased an organ for it for $75.00. S. Albert Wood served as the first pastor from 1905-1913.

After 1929, the meeting met mostly in the summer months for almost fifty years. In the 1930s, Eleanor Wood Whitman was the summer pastor. In the 1980s, as it became harder to find pastors for the summer, unprogrammed worship became the most common worship year-round at North Sandwich. Friends met for worship in the meetinghouse during the summer and in varied community sites the rest of the year.

An addition in 1993 allowed year-round use of the meetinghouse. It includes a smaller meeting room, two small classrooms, a utility room, and a dry kitchen. The older section of the meetinghouse, heated with a wood stove, is used primarily during the summer months. The new addition is wheelchair accessible and is heated with gas-heated coils in the cement slab under wooden flooring.

The meetinghouse is also used occasionally by others in the community for weddings and memorial services. Many acknowledge that the building transmits an abiding sense of peace, and the presence of a long procession of faithful friends. There is a burial ground just east of the building.

North Sandwich Friends Meetinghouse (with 1993 addition)

SOURCE: Evelyn S. Wallace of Tamworth, Jack Webb of Center Sandwich, Miriam Houston, and a booklet from the Center Sandwich Historical Society.

Hampton Friends Meetinghouse (1701)

Seabrook (formerly Hampton), New Hampshire
Erected: 1701
Location: Brown Road, Hampton Falls
Burial Ground: No
Private Residence

A monthly meeting was established here in 1699. The first recorded marriage among Friends in what was then Hampton took place at a special meeting in 1705 at the home of Thomas Bernard, where John Peaslee and Mary Martin were wed and forty-seven witnesses signed the marriage certificate. In 1701 a meetinghouse was built on land donated by Thomas Chace in a deed dated 6th month, 21st, 1701, at what is presently the southeast corner of the Elmwood Cemetery on U. S. Route 1. The cost was sixty-six pounds, four shillings, and the building originally measured twenty-six and a half feet wide by thirty-two feet long, and "eight feet at the stud."

This meetinghouse was used by Friends from Hampton, Salisbury, and also by Amesbury until that meeting built its own meetinghouse in 1705. The building presently stands on Brown Road in Hampton Falls. Now a residence, it bears a marker identifying it as a former Quaker meetinghouse.

A second meetinghouse was built in 1764 but was moved to another part of Seabrook, circa 1888. Used first as a shoe factory and later as a dance hall, it was eventually torn down.

SOURCE: *History of the Town of Hampton: 1638 to 1892* by Joseph Dow, 1938, Salem Press and Publishing Company. Reprinted in 1970 by Peter E. Randall, Publisher, Portsmouth, New Hampshire. Additional information provided by Eric Small, Seabrook Historical Society.

South Pittsfield Friends Meetinghouse

South Pittsfield, New Hampshire
Erected: 1863
Location: South Pittsfield Road, 3 miles north of
**   junction of Routes 202 and 107 S**
Burial Ground: Near site of earlier building
Currently Associated with Quakers

According to local history, the first Quaker in Pittsfield was Abram Green of Seabrook, New

Hampshire, who arrived prior to the Revolution, and was known locally locally for baking his neighbors' bread and beans in his outdoor oven. The first meetinghouse, which is reported to have had a gallery, is said to have been built in 1802 at the site of the Friends burial ground on present Berry Pond Road, on the upper slope of Catamount Mountain. It is said to have later burned.

The type of windows and the interior finish in the 1863 building indicate that alterations were probably made around the turn of the century. The attic contains an unusual wooden cranking mechanism for raising and lowering the shutters or room dividers. The building still is used by local groups, and is under the care of Weare Monthly Meeting, which meets there once or twice a year.

South Pittsfield Burial Ground

SOURCE: *History of Pittsfield* by E. Harold Young, 1953

Quaker City-Unity Friends Meetinghouse

Unity, New Hampshire
Erected: 1820
Location: 5 miles south of Claremont on Route
    12, 4.2 miles east on Unity Stage Road, and
    ¹/₁₀ mile south on Black North Road
Burial Ground: Yes
In Use as Quaker Meetinghouse

This meetinghouse, on an unpaved back road, has remained essentially unchanged since its construction, with the typical divided interior with swing-up shutters. The plastered walls and plain wainscoting exist in their original form. The benches are made of basswood, and there are three raised facing seats.

The left-hand door, which was originally the women's entrance, is wider than the men's right-hand entrance and was possibly built this way to accommodate the hoop skirts worn by women of that era. It is said that a fugitive from the law was once hidden in the attic by a Friend who believed him innocent. There is a small shed and outhouse to the right of the building, and the burial ground is to the left.

Local people and Friends from other meetings have done basic restoration work on the sills, roof and clapboarding.

Care of the building was legally transferred from Weare Monthly Meeting to the Quaker City–Unity Monthly Meeting a few years after the monthly meeting was established in 1993.

Unity Meetinghouse (Interior)

Unity Meeting Shed

SOURCE: *The Manchester Union Leader.* Henry T. Osborne.

Federated Church, Weare, New Hampshire

Weare, New Hampshire
Erected: 1795
Location: Quaker Street
Burial Ground: Yes
No Longer in Use as Quaker Meetinghouse

The first meetinghouse in Weare was in the center of town near the present town hall and was often used for town meetings. Two new meeting-houses—a North Meetinghouse and a South Meetinghouse—were built in 1795.

The North Meetinghouse had a platform at one end that made it possible to step directly out from a carriage, and there were two horse sheds on the property. In 1955 the building was sold and torn down, though the burial ground still remains at the front of the site.

The South Meetinghouse on Memorial Road in Clinton Grove was enlarged in 1813 to accommodate Quarterly Meeting. The building was torn down in 1916 and some of the materials were incorporated in the Drewry Bros. Toy Shop, which burned in 1936. That building was on what is now called Reservoir Drive at the bridge just below Lake Horace dam.

In the late 1800s a strong pastoral leaning developed in the meeting, and Friends and Congregationalists held joint services as the Weare Federated Church in a building (at the corner of Routes 114 and 177 in North Weare) that still stands. This arrangement ended in 1994 when the Congregationalists affiliated with a national Congregationalist body.

Three associated burial grounds are now under the care of the town.

Across from the South Cemetery is the site of the first Friends seminary (school) in New Hampshire, Clinton Grove. Moses Cartland of Lee Meeting was the first teacher there. A model of Clinton Grove Academy may be found at the Weare Historical Society, Route 114, Weare Center.

SOURCES: Henry Osborne and Elizabeth Straw

Above: Interior of Former North
Weare Meetinghouse
Left: Friends North Meetinghouse,
Weare (NLS)

Left: West Epping Friends Meetinghouse
Below: West Epping Friends Meetinghouse (Interior)

West Epping, New Hampshire
Erected: 1851
Location: Friend Street, off Route 27
Burial Ground: No
In Use as Quaker Meetinghouse

The first meetinghouse in West Epping is thought to have been built in the late 1700s. Although the bulk of the meeting records are missing, sold when the home of an elderly member was auctioned off, records indicate that the building was used "for more than fifty years before the present one was built in 1851." Presumably, Epping was then an allowed meeting under the care of the Seabrook, New Hampshire meeting. A Joshua Fulsom was a recorded minister in 1772, and a Fulsom was still a recorded minister as late as the 1950s.

The meeting in West Epping was closed for a period of time after the death of the minister, John Fulsom, but about twenty years ago, due to the interest of Miriam Jackson, it was reopened. The building was then under the care of Amesbury and Salem Quarter. In 1981 it was transferred to the care of Gonic Monthly Meeting, at which time it became a preparative meeting.

The building has been freshly painted, given a new roof, and carefully refurbished inside. It sits in a two-acre pine grove. Stone posts once used to hitch horses stand behind the building. The nearby cemetery has recently been cleaned up and its fence painted. Unprogrammed meeting for worship is held on alternate First Days.

SOURCE: Marion Marcotte and others.

Wolfeboro Friends Meetinghouse

Wolfeboro, New Hampshire
Erected: 1825
Location: North Main Street, Wolfeboro
Burial Ground: No
Private Residence

Local history reports that several Friends families, including the Varneys, Bassetts, and Nowells, moved to Wolfeboro at the close of the Revolutionary War, and that eventually there were enough Friends to warrant erecting a meetinghouse on the Varneys' lane at what is now the junction of Friend and North Maine Streets. For a number of years, meetings were held here on both First Day and at mid-week. The meeting-house was of traditional design, with facing benches and a dividing partition. Early records cite members Lindley M. Hoage and his wife Huldah as having a "special gift in ministry." An interesting note in the Wolfeboro town history records the style of bonnets worn by Quaker women in the early days: "They were regulated by the age of the wearer which was changeless; the aged women wearing odd shaped black silk,

middle-aged white silk of the same shape, and young misses white silk with the front slightly flaring."

It is not clear exactly when membership ebbed, but the meeting was laid down in 1851, and the house was sold that year. It was moved and presently stands as a residence on North Maine Street.

SOURCE: *History of Wolfeboro, New Hampshire* by Benjamin Franklin Parker, published by the town in 1901. Also, Louise Gehman, Director of Wolfeboro Public Library.

New Hampshire Meetinghouses No Longer Standing

Barrington, New Hampshire

New England Yearly Meeting archives list a meeting that existed in Barrington in 1775 but was laid down in 1783. The local town history states that there were Quakers in residence in 1768 when there was a dispute over paying taxes for the support of the Congregational minister.

An early map with no date indicates a number of churches but no meetinghouse, nor does the town history mention one. Louise Williams of the local historical society thinks it likely that Barrington Friends attended Dover meeting. However, according to Ms. Williams, hearsay has it that a meetinghouse existed for a short time on Locke Hill, on land owned by George S. Tuttle.

SOURCE: Silas Weeks, 8th month 1991.

Addendum: Notes in *The History of Rockingham County* say that "Quakers settled on Waldrons Hill in Barrington and built a Meetinghouse on land now owned by George S. Tuttle. Its dimensions or how long it was used are not known as it was taken away before the days of the oldest inhabitants now living."

I talked with Harlen Califf, who says that Locke Hill is part of Waldron Hill. Waldron Hill is where the present school and town office are located, Locke Hill being farther along on Route 126, past where it branches off of Route 9.

SOURCE: Silas Weeks, 3rd month, 1st, 1993.

Gilmanton Friends Meetinghouse

Gilmanton, New Hampshire

The site and cemetery are the only remnants of a Friends meeting here. The minutes of Dover Monthly Meeting mention that in 1903 the trustees were requested to look into disposing of the building; later it was reported that the members opposed that action. In 1910, when the matter was again raised, a motion to "rent to the Methodist people" was approved. In 1925 the subject of repairs to the building is mentioned in the minutes.

In 1930 the building was sold to Curtis Hidden Page, who lived down the street in a large brick house on the corner.

This building was the second on the site—the first structure having been razed about 1880. Records indicate that the meeting was first formed in 1780. A preparative meeting was established in 1814, at which time the first house may have been built. In 1815 a deed given by Jonathan and Jacob Rowe that transferred title to a half-acre parcel mentions the presence of a "meetinghouse." The burying ground located a short distance up Route 140 from the center of Gilmanton is under the care of the town. Dover Meeting transferred the title to the land to the town in 1992.

Gilmanton Friends burial ground

SOURCES: Elwyn Meader and H.L. Osler

Manchester, New Hampshire

In 1922 a city directory for Manchester listed a Friends church called Union Chapel at 63 South Elm Street. It was apparently organized in 1901 as a meeting place for orthodox Friends. The directory mentions that services were held at 10:15 a.m. and 7:00 p.m. Alice C. Winslow was the minister. Mrs. Donald Leitch served as clerk, Mary A. Chase as treasurer, and William P. Hall as sexton.

In 1928 there was no pastor named; in 1930, the last year the directory records Friends, the pastor was Harold N. Tollefson.

Mary A. Chase, as elder, appears to have been a mainstay of the meeting through 1922. Other names given are Mrs. Donald Leitch, Jessie Glover, William P. Hall, Mrs. Clarence Dolloff, Ella C. Johnson, Mrs. Agnes Muir, Gara E. Brown, Mrs. Robena Fuller, Ruth Pitman, Frank S. Fowler, and George R. Russell.

It is difficult to determine how many Friends who attended this meeting had migrated to the city from rural areas. At this writing, the date that this meeting was laid down is not known. The building was torn down and the site became a parking lot.

SOURCE: Shirley Leslie, Gonic Friends Meeting

New Durham, New Hampshire

Town history reports that there was a Friends meetinghouse on the southeasterly side of New Durham Ridge Road and the corner of what is presently called Quaker Road. A small lot there, which is shown on an 1856 town map, contains foundation stones. New England Yearly Meeting archives indicate there were two houses—the first built in 1809 and the second in 1817. The second building was removed and served for a while as a freight station on the nearby railroad; later it became part of a complex of buildings on State Highway 11 that are presently used for storage by the Cardinal Construction Company.

Some early Quaker families included Thomas Canney, Jr., who married Anna Meader of Rochester in 1787. A list of conscientious objectors who refused to serve in the New Durham militia in 1821 was prepared by the overseers and includes the names of Elijah Jenkins, James Canney, and Stephen Roberts. There is a Canney burying ground off the ridge in which the earliest burial date is 1829 and the last 1889. It is being restored

by the local historical society, as is the meetinghouse lot.

SOURCE: Eloise Bickford, town historian

Tamworth, New Hampshire
(see also Center Sandwich)

Records indicate that Sandwich Monthly
Meeting was established in 1802 and that a
meetinghouse was erected there between 1812-
1816. This building is reported to have been
removed to Tamworth in 1835, where it was long
known as the "Bean" Meetinghouse. It burned in
1849.

SOURCE: Evelyn S. Wallace, Tamworth, NH, 1986.

Quaker Burial Grounds in New Hampshire

Center Sandwich, New Hampshire—
Near Wentworth Hill.

Concord, New Hampshire—
Now a part of Old North Cemetery on State Street. Identified by marker.

Dover, New Hampshire—
On Sixth Street. Formerly the Meader family cemetery, now under the care of Gonic Friends.

Gilmanton, New Hampshire—
Short distance up Route 140 from Gilmanton Center. Under the care of the town.

Lee, New Hampshire—
Cartland family burial ground on North River Road in an open field across from the Cartland family homestead. The burying ground is well-maintained by the town of Lee.

Meaderboro, New Hampshire—
See Rochester, New Hampshire.

New Durham, New Hampshire—
On New Durham Ridge Road. Associated with the Canney family; used from 1829-1889.

North Sandwich, New Hampshire—
Just east of meetinghouse on Quaker-White-face Road.

Richmond, New Hampshire—
Near meetinghouse at Four Corners. Now maintained by local historical society.

Rochester, New Hampshire—
Across from Meaderboro meetinghouse. Under the care of Gonic Friends.

South Pittsfield, New Hampshire—
Near site of earlier meetinghouse on Berry Pond Road, on upper slope of Catamount Mountain.

Unity, New Hampshire—
On left as you face meetinghouse. Go five miles south of Claremont on Route 12, 4.2 miles east on Unity Stage Road, and 1/10 mile south on Black North Road.

Weare, New Hampshire—
Three burial grounds associated with Quakers and now under care of the town. One in front of site of North Weare meetinghouse at 2 Shady Hill Road (intersection of Memorial, Thorndike, and Shady Hill Roads); Friends North and New North cemeteries are at 216 Quaker Street.

Rhode Island

Rhode Island

R hode Island meetinghouses are especially interesting because they
vary in size from the largest in New England to several of the small-
est.

The "Great Meetinghouse" in Newport (built in 1699) is of historic interest
because of its size and partial early Jacobean structure. Before it was erected,
others were in existence in Newport. George Fox visited four meetings there in
1672.

For a complete history of the restoration of the Great Meetinghouse by the
Newport Historical Society, see their publication on the project. It contains
photos and prints of the building during various periods, as well as photos of
some of the restoration features and discusses the architectural, physical, techni-
cal, structural, and historic considerations in selecting 1807 as the date that
probably represented the most typical period of the restoration.

The present meeting in Providence is the largest in the state and has one of
the larger memberships in New England. Harold Myers had been minister at
Woonsocket in 1924 and gradually converted it to the nonpastoral form of
worship, helping to revive the Providence meeting.

A great deal of important information about the succession of earlier buildings and sites may be found in a paper written by Thyra Jane Foster and her
husband. The first meetinghouse in the area was built in 1719 in Smithfield; it
remained the principal meeting until the first Providence Meetinghouse was
built in 1725. The Fosters confirm the start-up process of the present meeting as
set forth by Myers. A paper by F. Warren Howe, Jr., contains information about
the structure and its fittings, as well as about the opening ceremony of the new
building.

Westerly Meeting (which prior to 1945 was named South Kingstown Meeting), at the extreme western edge of Rhode Island, possesses an excellent record
of its history that was presented to the local historical society in an address given
5th month, 13th, 1913, by a Mrs. E.B. Foster. Among other interesting things, Mrs.

Foster notes that an early meetinghouse on Tower Hill was attacked and destroyed by Indians, and that the deaths of the men, women, and children led to the battle in the Great Swamp, which ended King Philip's War. In 1743, the South Kingstown Monthly Meeting consisted of meetings in South Kingstown, Charlestown, Westerly, Hopkinton, and Richmond. Mrs. Foster's extensive report of the ups and downs of the various small meetings in Washington County includes the names of leading Friends and their families, as well as information about John Wilbur and a sketch of the Wilbur home. It covers the period leading up to 1879, the date of construction of the present meetinghouse in Westerly on Elm Street.

The only other meetinghouse built on an island that I can think of, besides those on Nantucket, is Conanicut, on Jamestown Island; Conanicut is also called the "Jamestown meeting." It is a small, well-maintained house on a small, walled lot. My understanding is that this location may be different from the first site on what is now Eldred Avenue, where there is a small Friends burying ground. Philadelphia Friends summering on the island reopened the house in 1973. In 1976, with matching funds from the Rhode Island Preservation Fund, some necessary restoration took place, including the replacement of some Victorian-period doors.

Ethyl Rosenbalm, a member of the historical society in Kingstown, writes that there was a meetinghouse in Wakefield that later became a Seventh Day Adventist Church and is now a private residence. I have not followed this up.

Cathrine Hull of the Clark Memorial Library in Carolina, Rhode Island, was kind enough to send me information about a former meetinghouse located at Usquepaugh, a delightful rural place where I often stop when I'm in the area to buy stone-ground flour at the old water-driven Kenyon Mill. The last meeting held in that meetinghouse was a funeral in 1844.

The history of East Greenwich records that quarterly meeting in that part of the state at one time consisted of Portsmouth, Newport, and Fall River. In the spring, when it was held in East Greenwich, Friends arrived at the foot of Queen Street by boat. There was an academy, possibly run by Friends, whose students flocked to the landing to greet the Quakers when the bell was rung announcing their arrival. So many people turned out on these occasions that the town dubbed them "Quaker days."

The meetinghouse at Little Compton is one of my favorites. Both its interior and its exterior have been lovingly restored by the local historical society.

Rhode Island Meetinghouses

Arnold Mills Friends Meetinghouse

Arnold Mills, Rhode Island
Erected: 1810
Location: Hillside Road and
    Abbott Run Valley Road
Burial Ground: no
Not in Use as Quaker Meetinghouse

The first Quaker in Arnold Mills was Ebenezer Metcaff, who had a machine shop there that did work for America's early textile mills. Metcaff was a major contributor to the Moses Brown School, a Friends school in Providence, Rhode Island.

The meetinghouse at Arnold Mills is a two-story building originally with galleries, built in 1810 by James Smith. By the early 1900s, the attendance had dwindled, and the building became a part-time meeting place for the Blackstone Valley Girl Scouts. A full second floor later replaced the galleries.

The meetinghouse was later purchased for use as a community center, and in 1942 the Arnold Mills Community House Trust was formed. This organization made a provision that the Society of Friends might continue to use the building, even though they were not a community organization.

SOURCE: Anne Humes, from records at the Cumberland County Library: *Cumberland Rhode Island Historical Story*, 3rd edition, 1976, and *North Cumberland, a History* by Robert V. Simpson, 1975.

Jamestown Friends Meetinghouse

Conanicut (Jamestown) Rhode Island
Erected: circa 1710
Location: North Road and Weeden Lane
Burial Ground: Yes (at original site on Eldred
    Avenue)
In Use as Quaker Meetinghouse (summers only)

Conanicut Meetinghouse is a small, well-maintained building on a walled lot. It was moved from Eldred Avenue, Jamestown, where a burial ground remains, to its present site in 1733, and enlarged to twice its original size in 1786. From 1777 to 1782, the meetinghouse was occupied and used as a hospital by British soldiers, and the graves of seven soldiers remain nearby. The meeting was laid down in 1891. In 1973 the building was listed in the National Register as "within the Windmill Hill historic district." It has been used by vacationing Friends as a meetinghouse in summers since that year, and some restoration work was done in 1976 with the help of The Rhode Island Preservation Society.

SOURCE: Deborah Lutman.

Little Compton Meetinghouse (Restored, 1963)

Little Compton, Rhode Island
Erected: 1700
Location: West Main Road
Burial Ground: Yes
Not in Use as Quaker Meetinghouse

Many of the materials from the original Little Compton Meetinghouse were incorporated in the second meetinghouse built in 1815. This later building was remodeled and "improved" in 1870 with large doors, windows and a vestibule, but with few interior changes. The present two-story meetinghouse measures twenty-two by thirty feet. Meeting for worship was finally discontinued in 1903 when the sole attendee for the previous twenty years died. The meetinghouse was later taken over by the Little Compton Historical Society and in 1963 completely and beautifully restored to its 1815 condition.

The burial ground to the rear of the building is open to the public in August and is well worth a visit.

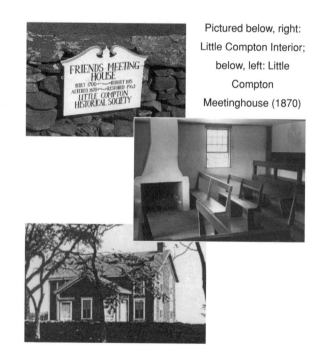

Pictured below, right: Little Compton Interior; below, left: Little Compton Meetinghouse (1870)

SOURCE: Carlton C. Brownell, Little Compton Historical Society.

Evangelical Friends Church of Newport

Middletown, Rhode Island
Erected: 1972
Location: 70 Bliss Mine Road, Middletown
Burial Ground: No
In Use as Quaker Church

In 1657, eleven Friends sailed to America from London; six of the group continued on to Newport. In 1699 work on a large meetinghouse was begun (see Newport, Rhode Island). In 1922, when the Great Meetinghouse was sold to the Community Center Association of Newport, the Newport Friends built a new brick church building and parsonage at 21 Farewell Street (very close to the old meetinghouse). The ministry in this new meetinghouse began with Reverend Andrew Starbuck.

It is important to note that in the early 1800s, Newport Friends were influenced by the preaching of Joseph John Gurney, who led the way to a stronger emphasis upon the scriptures as the final authority for faith and practice. This led to a more evangelical emphasis for Newport Friends. In 1951, some of the former members of Portsmouth Friends and Newport Friends affiliated with the Ohio Yearly Meeting. In 1961, the church officially joined the Ohio Yearly Meeting (EFC). The first monthly meeting of the newly named "Evangelical Friends Church of Newport, Rhode Island" took place on 21 September 1961.

In 1970, the meetinghouse and parsonage at 21 Farewell Street were sold to the Newport Historical Society due to general disrepair and need for a better location.

An interim worship site was established with the Calvary Methodist Church on Annandale Road in Newport. In 1971, nearly three acres of land was located and secured in nearby Middletown in sight of the Atlantic Ocean and adjacent to Green End Pond. Ground breaking for the church was September 5, 1971, with a dedication service on 17 September 1972. The Reverend Calvin Gordon was the first pastor in the new building.

Renovations have taken place over the years with a major renovation in the downstairs level in 1994-1997. Since 1995/6, the Aquidneck Island Christian Academy School has shared the downstairs with the church. In 1997-98, a parsonage was built.

A 25th anniversary dinner and open house took place during 12-14 September, 1997.

SOURCE: Neal Flower.

Newport Friends Meetinghouse
"The Great Meetinghouse" (Present, after restoration)

Newport, Rhode Island
"The Great Meetinghouse"
Erected: 1699
Location: Corner of Farewell and Marlborough
    Streets
Burial Ground: Yes
Now a Quaker Site in a Historical District

The original Great Friends Meetinghouse is the oldest surviving house of worship in Newport. Use of the grounds of the Friends Meetinghouse by Europeans began in 1639 with the construction of Nicholas Easton's house, facing Farewell Street, and other necessary barns, stables, and outbuildings. Easton's first house burned in 1641, but he built another, which he bequeathed to Newport's Friends upon his death in 1676. This house probably became the Friends' first permanent place of worship.

George Fox visited four meetings here on his visit to America in 1672.

Construction of the Great Meetinghouse was authorized in 1689, and began in 1699. It was essentially a Jacobean structure with medieval framing. The original girders, which span a forty-five foot opening, are still in place. The original roof was of "hip" construction, topped by a cupola. This construction was changed when the "south" meetinghouse was added in 1807. This addition was nearly equal in size to the "great" meetinghouse and contained a balcony on three sides. The "north" meeting, a two-story structure, was added in 1729 (according to meeting minutes, "for the conveniency of the women's meeting"), and its second floor room accessed the "great" meetinghouse. Other enlargements were made in 1858 and 1867. During the first few decades of the eighteenth century, it was the largest and most recognizable building in town, and throughout the 1700s appeared as a landmark in maps and painted landscapes of Newport.

Newport Friends Meetinghouse (Before restoration)

The annual New England Yearly Meeting, with attendance as high as three thousand in some years, was held in the Great Meetinghouse many times up until 1903. The building was sold in 1922, and was used as a community recreation center. It became an important meeting place for the African-American community and it was here that the Martin Luther King Center, a social service agency now located across the street, was founded.

The Newport Historical Society acquired the building in 1967. Between 1967 and 1975 it was restored to its 1807 appearance under the guidance of architect Orin M. Bullock.

SOURCE: *The Restoration of the Great Meetinghouse at Newport, Rhode Island 1699-1974* by Ester Fisher Benson. Published by the Newport Historical Society and the Newport Historical Society web site, www.newporthistorical.org

Portsmouth Friends Meetinghouse

Portsmouth, Rhode Island
Erected: 1700
Location: 11 Middle Road
Burial Ground: Yes
In Use as Quaker Meetinghouse
National Register of Historic Places

This structure, and the one in nearby Newport, are two of the oldest Quaker meetinghouses still standing in New England, and, indeed, in all America. The hip roof is most unusual. In 1657, English Friends landed at Founders Rock near Portsmouth; they established the Rhode Island Monthly Meeting in 1658, which included Portsmouth and Newport.

George Fox visited the meeting when he came to America in 1672.

In 1692, Portsmouth Friends purchased a lot, two-and-a-half by six rods, and the house on it from Robert Hodgson to be used as a meeting-house. Meeting minutes of 8th mo., 17th, 1699 read, "Friends have laid out and appointed the place where the meeting house shall stand, and have brought great stones and other stones to lay the foundation."

In 1700 the old meetinghouse was sold to Joseph Mosey and proceeds were applied to the new meetinghouse. Sheds were built for horses in 1701. In 1703, John Warner, a Friend from North Carolina, kept a private school in the meeting-house. In 1705 an addition was build for the convenience of the Women's Meeting.

The building housed British and Hessian troops during the Revolution, when nearby Aquidneck Island was occupied. Powder was stored in the basement. Meeting minutes of 12th mo., 30th, 1776 read, "As our meeting house hath at this time a number of soldiers in it, it renders it inconvenient to proceed to business, therefore this meeting is adjourned to the breaking up of the meeting for worship at Newport next 5th day." The occupation caused much economic hardship, and many Friends left the area.

In 1784 Friends established a school near here, but due to hard times, it only lasted four years. The remaining funds were entrusted to Moses Brown, and eventually a school in his name was established in Providence.

A keystone in the fireplace dates the remodeling of the meetinghouse at 1887. Changes included sheathing the exposed interior beams with finished lumber, installing new pews and pulpit furniture, building a new partition between the men's and women's sides, adding window shutters, balcony railing, and installing new coat hook boards and fireplaces. Major exterior changes included removal of the original, separate entry vestibules for men and women and the construction of the present entry hall. One of the original entry rooms now serves as the basement entry on the north side of the building. Also added at this time was the porch on the south side and its adjoining privy. Fireplaces were replaced as the means of heat with the installation of a furnace in the basement.

In 1890 the meeting called Seth C. Rees to be the first paid full time pastor.

Electric lights were installed in 1900. In the hurricane of 1938, the west section of the sheds was so badly damaged that they were demolished. The north section stood until about 1960 when this was demolished. In 1958—the meeting's 300th anniversary, the basement was excavated to make room for a larger Sunday School and meeting room, kitchen, nursery, and two bathrooms. The south porch was remodeled for an office in 1972. There is a burial ground to the rear of the building.

The meetinghouse is now the site of the Portsmouth Evangelical Friends Church.

Portsmouth (old photo)

Portsmouth interior

SOURCE: Rhode Island Preservation Commission and Jordan Jacobson, pastor of the Portsmouth Evangelical Friends Church and the church's web site, www.friendschurch.com

Providence Friends Meetinghouse
Providence Friends Meetinghouse (third, NLS)

Providence Friends Meetinghouse (fourth; present)

Providence, Rhode Island
Erected: 1954-55
Location: 99 Morris Avenue
Burial Ground: No
In Use as Quaker Meetinghouse

The first meetinghouse in the Providence area was built at Smithfield, in 1703, and it remained the principal meeting until the Providence

meetinghouse was built. The first meetinghouse in Providence was built in 1725, probably on Stamner's Hill. A second lasted until 1844, when it was removed as a dwelling and later torn down. A new and third house was built on the site of the second and lasted until 1951, when it was sold to the city; an apartment building now occupies the site. The present or fourth meetinghouse house is a brick structure built in 1954-55 on land at the rear of the Moses Brown School. Thomas Perry headed the building committee and Albert Harkness was the architect. A dedication talk was given by Alexander Purdy in September of 1952.

SOURCE: Thyra Jane Foster and Judith Lewis.

Saylesville Friends Meetinghouse

Saylesville (Lincoln) Rhode Island
Erected: 1703
Location: Great Road at River Road
Burial Ground: Yes (2)
In Use as Quaker Meetinghouse

The oldest section of this structure was built

in 1703; the present main part was added about forty years later. The interior is exposed post and beam construction. The building was used as a school during part of the eighteenth century. Job Scott, teacher, minister, and writer, was a prominent Friend in the community. The Saylesville Friends have been holding meetings continuously for 250 years. It is a preparative meeting of Providence Monthly Meeting.

A stone mounting-block still exists, and the well-tended burial ground is in the meetinghouse yard.

SOURCE: Robert N. Cool and Bruce Downing.

Smithfield Friends Meetinghouse

Woonsocket, Rhode Island
Erected: 1881
Location: 108 Smithfield Road
Burial Ground: Yes
In Use As Quaker Meetinghouse

A Providence Preparative Meeeting was held at what became Saylesville, Rhode Island begin-

ning in 1705 under Greenwich Monthly Meeting. This was set of a Providence Monthly Meeting in 1718. The name became Smithfield Monthly Meeting in 1731, when the town of Smithfield was formed from Providence. In 1783, the meeting split into four sections: Smithfield Monthly Meeting (at "upper Smithfield"), Uxbridge Monthly Meeting, Providence Monthly Meeting, and Lower Smithfield Constituent Meeting (the Saylesville Meeting, now under the new Providence Monthly Meeting). Smithfield Monthly Meeting has been held since 1719 in what is now Woonsocket, Rhode Island.

Descendants of Richard Arnold, one of the first settlers in the area in the mid-1600s, were forefathers of the town of Woonsocket and built the first Quaker meetinghouse there in 1719. For more than one hundred years in Woonsocket there was no place of public worship except the Friends meetinghouse.

Friends in the area also took the initiative in education. Among the excellent private schools were the Thornton Academy (founded by a Quaker preacher of that name) and The Friends School in Providence, now named Moses Brown School for its founder.

The 1719 meetinghouse was made twenty feet square. It was enlarged in 1755 by and ell twenty by thirty feet. In 1755 this ell was removed and an addition thirty-two feet square was built. In 1849 the entire building was remodeled, later adding green blinds. It remained thus until destroyed by fire in 1881.

Among early family names in Smithfield Friends Meeting are Arnold, Aldrich, Ballou,

Smithfield Friends
Meetinghouse
(1719-1881)

Mowry, Smith, Steere, Paine, Farnum, Comstock, Thayer, Lapham, Kelley, and Buffum. Stephen Hopkins, one of the signers of the Declaration of Independence, was a member of the meeting but was removed from membership for keeping a slave.

Members of Smithfield Monthly Meeting were active in the anti-slavery movement. Arnold Buffum, the first president of the New England Anti-Slavery Society was eventually disowned by the meeting because he would not stop his public lecturing against slavery. He continued to attend the meeting with his children.

The meetinghouse that now stands upon the original land purchase of 1713 was erected in 1881 immediately after the fire. News of the disaster came to the congregation while assembled in quarterly meeting. Rebuilding took just a few months; the fire was on May 12 and the meeting

was reassembled in the new meetinghouse on November 10. The present parsonage next to the meetinghouse was erected in 1924.

Among ministers who served the meeting between 1881 and 1932 were Abel C. Monroe, Jesse McPherson, Harry R. Hole, Levinus K. Painter, Elgar J. Pennington, Jesse Stanfield, D. Elton Trueblood, Harold W. Myers, and Paul L. Sturgis.

Alongside the meetinghouse is a Friends Cemetery, which includes the grave of Mary Miles, a child born to fugitive slaves who were sheltered by a member of the meeting. That cemetery has not been used since the 1940s. Across the road from the meetinghouse and parsonage is the town's Union Cemetery, which also includes Quaker graves.

Source: *Smithfield Meeting of Friends,* published for the meeting's 213th anniversary.

Westerly Friends Meetinghouse

Westerly, Rhode Island
Erected: 1879
Location: 57 Elm Street
Burial Ground: Yes (in Hopkinton, R.I.)
In Use as Quaker Meetinghouse

The present meetinghouse in Westerly was known as the South Kingstown Monthly Meeting prior to the 1945 reunification of Friends in New England. South Kingstown Meeting was the home meeting of John Wilbur and in 1845 was at the center of the division of New England Friends into the Wilburite, or Conservative Friends, and the Gurneyites, known as "the larger body." This meetinghouse, built in 1879, served as the yearly meeting for the Wilburite Friends prior to the reunification. Meetings in Westerly were held at the home of Charles Perry beginning around 1854; most of the attenders were connected with Wilburite Friends in Hopkinton. The new meetinghouse was built in 1879 or property belonging to Charles Perry.

South Kingstown Meeting was set off from Greenwich Monthly Meeting in 1743 and consisted over the years of preparative meetings held in Hopkinton, Richmond, South Kingstown (variously in the villages of Kington, Peace Dale, Wakefield, and Perryville), and Westerly.

An early meetinghouse in South Kingstown at Tower Hill was attached and destroyed by the Narragansetts and Wampanoags during King Philip's War, an Indiana uprising in 1675 and 1676 prompted by the seizing of Indian lands by Europeans. The attach may have led to the battle in the Great Swamp, which brought King Philip's War to an end.

The first meetinghouse in Westerly was built in 1743 on the north side of Post Road, a short distance northeast of Dunn's Corners, where a Friends burial ground may still be found. There is also a Friends burial ground in South Kingstown—at the meetinghouse site on Tower Hill Road in the village of Wakefield, and another in South Kingstown at the site of the Western Meeting on Old Post Road in the village of Perryville. The Westerly Meeting burial ground is in Hopkinton at the site of the first meetinghouse of the Hopkinton Preparative Meeting.

SOURCE: Edward D. Baker

Rhode Island Meetinghouses No Longer Standing

Greenwich Friends Meetinghouse

East Greenwich, Rhode Island

The first meetinghouse in East Greenwich was built on land belonging to John Spencer near Payne's Pond. It was started in 1701 and completed in 1703 on what is presently Cedar Avenue, where there is still a Friends cemetery. One contribution made towards the cost of construction was a hog valued at 1 pound, 8s, 6p. Expenses included 9s for rum for the raising and 10s-6p for beer.

This structure was replaced in 1804 by a large two-story building located on Pierce Street next to Kent Academy. It was torn down in 1952, an act that upset local history buffs. The town hall parking lot now occupies the site.

SOURCE: *The Tercentenary Book, 1677 to 1977,* East Greenwich, Rhode Island. Debby Nunes, research librarian, East Greenwich Free Library.

Hopkinton, Rhode Island

Over the years three meetinghouses were constructed in Hopkinton, although none are still standing. The Hopkinton Preparative Meeting, a constituent meeting of the South Kingstown Monthly Meeting, built its first meetinghouse about 1743 on property that is now the burial ground of Westerly Monthly Meeting on Keuhn Road. This building was dismantled when a new meetinghouse was constructed in 1832 across the street at the junction of Keuhn Road and Clark's Fall Road (a private residence now stands on this site). With the division of Friends in New England in 1845, the Gurneyite faction barred the door to the Wilburite faction, and so the Wilburites built a new meetinghouse less than a mile away on Clark's Falls Road.

John Wilbur is buried in the burial ground along with many members of the Collins, Foster, and Henderson families. John Wilbur's house, and Underground Railroad Station, is located nearby.

SOURCE: Edward D. Baker

South Kingstown, Rhode Island

My source for this information is Caroline Hazard's *Narragansett Friends Meetings, 1900,* but much of the data is confused or at odds with itself. Friends did come to Rhode Island from the ship Woodhouse, and George Fox did visit there in 1672. My impression was that George Fox established the South Kingstown Meeting, but Ms. Hazard does not note any record of meetings prior to 1698.

The South Kingstown Meeting split off from

the Greenwich Meeting in 1743, but already had its own meetinghouse in 1700, described as having stood on the southern spur of Tower Hill about a mile from the village of Wakefield, on land sold to Thomas Hazard in 1698 by a person named Seward. A marker dates the site as the location of a Quaker meetinghouse in 1700, though only the burying ground remains. Hazard says that a Friend visiting there in 1706 made note of a thirty by thirty-six-foot building.

The site is just off the southbound edge of U.S. Route 1, where the road from Wakefield, Old Tower Hill Road, enters the highway. A marker erected by the Pettaquamscutt Historical Society is located on the site.

Old Quaker Cemetery , South Kingstown

SOURCE: Silas Weeks, 5th month 1990. Also, Edward D. Baker.

Usquepaugh, Rhode Island

Usquepaugh is a small settlement located partly in the town of Richmond and partly in South Kingstown.

It is locally recorded that in 1755 John Knowles deeded an acre of land for "the use and privilege of a people called Quakers" where they built a meetinghouse. The last known use of the building was for a funeral in 1844; the building was later sold. The cemetery, deeded to the town of Richmond in 1899, is located just south of the village on Kingston Road, Route 138.

SOURCE: *Driftways Into The Past: Local History of the Town of Richmond, Rhode Island*, published by the Richmond Historical Society, 1977. Additional information supplied by Catherine C. Hull, clerk, Memorial Library, Carolina, Rhode Island.

Western Friends Meeting
Wakefield, Rhode Island
(village center of South Kingstown)

The site of another meetinghouse in South Kingstown is preserved as a burial ground maintained by the town. Western Preparative Meeting, a constituent meeting of South Kingstown Monthly Meeting, constructed a meetinghouse on this site in 1750. It was dismantled in 1888. The burial ground is located in the Perryville section of town on Old Post Road between Gravely Hill Road and the junction with U.S. Route 1, the Oliver Hazard Perry Memorial Highway. Among the families represented in this burial ground are Perry, Card, Watson, Browning, Knowles, and Church.

SOURCE: Edward D. Baker.

Quaker Burial Grounds in Rhode Island

Conanicut Island (Jamestown), Rhode Island—
On Eldred Avenue, at original site of meetinghouse.

East Greenwich, Rhode Island—
On Cedar Avenue.

Hopkinton, Rhode Island—
Kuehn Road, off Clarks Falls Road. John Wilbur is buried there, and his house is nearby.

Jamestown, Rhode Island—
See Conanicut, Rhode Island.

Little Compton, Rhode Island—
In rear of meetinghouse; open in August.

Newport, Rhode Island—
Near "Great Meetinghouse."

Perryville, South Kingstown, Rhode Island—
Old Post Road, west of Gravelly Hill Road.

Portsmouth, Rhode Island—
Behind meetinghouse.

Saylesville, Rhode Island—
In meetinghouse yard.

South Kingstown, Rhode Island—
On southern spur of Tower Hill, marker there mentions a meetinghouse was there in 1700. The burial ground is in the village of Wakefield where Old Tower Hill Road connects with U.S. Route 1.

Westerly, Rhode Island—
North side of the Post Road, northeast of Dunn's Corners.

Vermont

Vermont

When I started work on Vermont meetinghouses, one of the first people I contacted was Tom Bassett, then clerk of the New England Yearly Meeting Archives Committee. He suggested that I look at an article called "Early Quaker Meetinghouses in Vermont" by C.W. Hughes and A.D. Bradley in the July 1961 issue of *Vermont History*. There I found the following listing of meetinghouse locations and dates: Danby, 1782; Mt. Holly, 1803; (East) Montpelier, 179_; North Ferrisburg, 179_; Monkton, 1801; Varneys Corner, 1861; Monkton Ridge, 1878; Weybridge, 181_; Starksboro, 1812; South Starksboro Creek, 1871; Lincoln, 1810; Grand Isle West Shore, 1795; and Grand Isle, 1827.

He attached a copy of a memorandum of title regarding the Mechanicsville Cemetery, where in 1849 Samuel Cook, on behalf of Friends, leased the burying ground to Austin Morgan for "As long as wood grows and water runs." Morgan agreed to "make two rods of wall each year until a wall is built on the east, north, and west sides of said tract and otherwise improve and take care of said premises in a good and husband like manner and suffer no injury to graves or gravestones..."

Another source I contacted early on was the Vermont Historical Society in Montpelier, asking about the former East Montpelier Meetinghouse. They replied, using a standard form that started out as follows: "Thank you for your interest in Vermont history. We hope that a mere "X" as a form of communication will not keep stereotyping us Vermonters as terse, stoic, one-syllable Yankees. The truth of the matter is that we are swamped with requests like yours and we have only a very small staff. We hope that you will be able to come to Montpelier someday so that we can greet you with a smile and a "Hello" and not an "X."

Wealtha Baker Bardosy responded with a nice note when I inquired about the Weybridge Meetinghouse. She wrote, "The only cemetery that I know is here behind our home. It is known as Quaker Village Cemetery and that is the original title of this Village. I remember my mother telling me a few tales about people who lived here that were Quakers. A Samuel Meeker used to draw from her uncle's well. All of a sudden, he stopped. He told Mom's uncle that he could not take water from the well, as another man, who also drew water there, had come home the night before drunk and he would not drink water from the same well as he did."

She continued, "As near as I can find, a group of Quakers settled here around 1780. An article states that one of the first settlers at the Lower Falls was Samuel Meeker who built a woolen mill there. He was joined by others of the same faith, and the settlement became known as Quaker Village. The name still persists, but all that is left of the original group is a small Quaker cemetery near the river. Most stones have gone under the soil, but there are only two with markings. Among the early settlers was a group of Quakers who built a church on what is Fields Day Road near the border of land in the town of New Haven. A few years later, the church burned and a new one was built in the village. That too was destroyed by fire and the Methodist Church was built on the same foundation. That church was torn down a few years ago. I still own the land where the first church was built and my grandfather was deeded the cemetery with the hopes it would be cared for. The 'Old Cemetery Association of Vermont' sees to it."

Sandra Rhodes of the Lincoln town office supplied information about a meetinghouse in Lincoln. She said, "I have done a lot of searching for where this house is in Bristol now. One person tells me one place and another person another, so I have not found it for sure. As for a foundation still being there, I'm not sure if it is or not. We have far too much snow to go and look now. The Friends Cemetery is still there. Our town pays to have the grass and brush cut in the summer. I went up one time and wrote down most of the names on the stones. It grew dark before I got to the last two rows. I hope to go back and finish it this spring. We have one street in Lincoln still called Quaker Street. In fact, this Town Office is on Quaker Street. I have been told it was once called Mud Flat."

Regarding Monkton Friends in Addison County, Joseph Hoag was the first to arrive, coming from New York state in 1797. As other Friends settled in the area, Hoag reported, "We have lived to see, to our great comfort, seven preparative meetings, three monthly meetings, and a quarterly meeting settled in this county. In the first two years, we used to walk over four miles twice a week—spring, summer, and fall. In winter, I used my oxen for a team, taking all the family with us. Starting about sunrise, we could get to meeting seasonably and [be] home about sunset. When I was able to buy and keep a horse for my wife to ride,I felt rich."

In East Montpelier, a record exists of a Friend who fell from grace, then asked that his membership be reinstated: "Dear Friends, I sometime past, thru ungardness (sic), agreed to provide a dinner for a Captain and his company on a training field day which I provided accordingly and I am sensible that I have infringed on Friends principles and testimony against militia affairs for which I am sorry and do condemn and desire Friends to pass by my offense and continue me under your care." Signed, Johnson Gove.

I asked my stepdaughter, Joanna, to see what she could find out about the existence of a meetinghouse in Hartland, Vermont, as she lived nearby. A Mr. Motschman told her that papers for the year of 1906 listed a Friends cemetery at Hartland Four Corners with twenty-six graves ranging in dates from 1801 to 1906, but that there was no record of a meetinghouse.

Many Vermont Friends maintained a firm commitment to the Society's peace testimony. Cyrus Guerney Pringle was conscripted into the Union Army in 7th month, 13th, 1863. He could have paid a $300 fine and have been released but refused to do so. Along with other conscientious objectors, he was sent to the Vermont 4th Regiment, where they refused to do service. After much hardship, their case was presented to President Abraham Lincoln, who said it was his wish that they be sent home immediately.

With the help of Elizabeth Moger, former archivist of New York Yearly Meeting, I was able to identify and visit the sites of all former meetinghouses and burying grounds once under the care of New York Yearly Meeting, except for South Lincoln, which was the site of Creek Meeting. These visits in the summer of 1995 allowed me to meet and speak with Bertha Hanson, who had sent me material on Weybridge meeting and burial ground. I also visited Sandra Rhodes of the Lincoln town office; she had sent me photos of the former Lincoln structure, the remains of which I was eventually able to trace. The priest at Our Lady of Mt. Carmel Catholic Church in East Charlotte sent me a helpful letter about a structure that had been removed from Starksboro.

Vermont Meetinghouses

Burlington Friends Meetinghouse (left), Bassett House (right)

Burlington, Vermont
Established, 1958; building dates to 1851
Location: 173 North Prospect Street
Burial Ground: No
In Use As Quaker Meetinghouse

This relatively new meeting was established in 1958. The meetinghouse itself was formerly a carriage house that was built in 1851 and owned by a Thaddius Fletcher. Meetings were first held in the building in 1962. Hardwood flooring from the former Bethany Congregational Church in Montpelier, Vermont, was put in when the building was converted. William R. Huntington designed additions in 1982, which included an enlarged meeting room and space for pre-school children.

Since 1995, the meeting has owned Bassett House. The meeting uses first floor of Bassett House for First Day school activities and also rents the space for day use to community groups.

Two apartments on the upper floor provide rental income. At some point the meeting plans to make space available as hospitality for traveling Friends and to accommodate weekend workshops.

SOURCE: Thomas D. S. Bassett, Clerk of Meeting

Former Starksboro Friends Meetinghouse,
(now Our Lady of Mount Carmel Church)

Charlotte, Vermont
(former Starksboro and now East Charlotte)
Erected: 1812
Location: 2894 Spear Street, Charlotte
Burial Ground: No
No Longer in Use as Quaker Meetinghouse

In reply to my written inquiry about the meetinghouse here, the town library sent me the following information.

"Nestled along a row of trees near Baptist Corners in East Charlotte is the second oldest Catholic Church and oldest in continuous use in Vermont. It is a church of the old style; white sided with tall double doors—it stands as it has since 1858 (local Catholics in 1853 recognized the need for a church. In 1858, they purchased a residence and converted part of it into a chapel.) Then it was learned that ten miles away in Starksboro, Vermont, an abandoned Quaker Meetinghouse was for sale. Built in 1812, it had been used for over forty years by a group of Quakers who had moved west. The Charlotte Catholics purchased the building and waited until the winter of 1858-1859 to move the structure to Charlotte."

One report says that "Materials were carried to Charlotte to be remodeled, but lore of the Church has it that the Meetinghouse was moved the whole ten miles on skids by oxen."

In 1874 funds were raised for interior furnishings, painting, and new windows. In 1880 a bell tower and bell were added. In 1966 and again in 1976, major interior and exterior renovations were made, including vinyl siding, a new stairway to the balcony, a refurbished bell tower, and new doors.

Fr. Gerald Ragio, parish priest, writes, "I am told that the house was cut into two pieces and that one can see the saw marks in the basement—I haven't crawled in there to see for myself." He adds, "I believe that it is quite appropriate that after the Quakers moved west, that their building continues to be a Holy space and a place for worship and that we Catholics will be worthy in our lives of its history."

Fr. Ragio believes that buildings take on something of the spirit of those who used them. He notes that the Catholic Carmelite tradition is also one of waiting and ruminating on the word of God, not so far from the worship practice of the Quakers who built the meetinghouse. He says that visitors often comment that there is a special feeling in the building. "Prayer, silence, and waiting on God can't help but be imbued in the wood."

SOURCE: *Our Lady of Mount Carmel, Charlotte, Vermont—125 Years; 1858 to 1983* by Carole Novick; Gerald Ragio, parish priest.

Monkton Ridge Friends Meetinghouse

Monkton Ridge, Vermont
Location: Monkton Ridge Road
 (also Silver Street)
Burial Ground: Yes, about two miles north of
 town center; another in the town is privately
 maintained
No Longer in Use as Quaker Meetinghouse

The first record of Quaker ministry in Monkton, Vermont, was made by Joseph Hoag, who arrived in 1789 when there were only three Quaker families in the area, but later wrote: "We have to our great comfort lived to see the county contain seven Preparative Meetings, three Monthly Meetings, and one Quarterly Meeting."

The first request for a formal meeting was made 9th month, 11th, 1795 in the home on Nicholas Holmes of Monkton, Vermont. In 1804 this became an established monthly meeting. In 1811, two acres were purchased from Nathan Hoag and Jonathan Holmes for $40. A one-story meetinghouse with dividing partition was erected. The burial ground can still be found on the old road past the Rotax Farm. One day while Joseph Hoag was plowing, he had a vision that predicted the Civil War, an experience which later established his leadership among Friends.

By 1860 the meetinghouse was in need of repair and was moved to Varney's Corners in Charlotte, Vermont. The old site was then sold.

In 1870 attendance at Varney's Corners was falling. It was decided on 11th month, 2nd, 1877, to acquire a site on Monkton Ridge. On 3rd month, 6th, 1878, a deed for the present property was secured from John Bushey for $150. Eighty dollars from the laid-down meeting on Grand Isle was added to other funds, and the meetinghouse, with a seating capacity of 250, was completed in the fall of 1878 at a cost of $1,200. In 1919 a portico was added to the front of the building, and the membership was substantial enough to warrant the building of the present parsonage. Improvements—including a new ceiling, wiring, an unfinished basement, a First Day schoolroom, and a furnace—were made in 1954 at a cost of $729. Professor Necheri of Montreal, Canada, created a memorial stained glass window for the meeting-

house, using ancient European methods. Special chimes from the electric organ ring in the village at Easter and Christmas.

The meeting was laid down in 1997. The building, still owned by New York Yearly Meeting, is used by a Methodist congregation and is known as the Friends–Methodist Church.

SOURCE: *A Meeting Place Can Talk About the Past*, by Bertha Hanson, August, 1981 (supplied by Deborah Chamberlin, town librarian).

Plainfield Friends Meetinghouse

Plainfield, Vermont
Erected: 1993
Location: 203 Martin Meadow Road
Burial Ground: No
In Use as Quaker Meetinghouse

There are two entrance doors to this simple frame, cape-type structure. The left door leads to the meeting room, which occupies the full width of the building, and the right one to the utility services and library. There is a full basement with Sunday School rooms that open to the exterior slope of the site.

The total cost of land and building is estimated at $155,000. Alan Walker was clerk of the building committee.

Putney Friends Meetinghouse

Putney, Vermont
Erected: 1985-86
Location: Exit 4 off Route 91, Route 5N one mile, turn left into meeting parking lot.
Burial Ground: No
In Use as Quaker Meetinghouse

Construction began on this building in the summer of 1985 on an acre of land donated by Constance St. John. Andrew St. John was the architect, and Sheridan Bartlett the general contractor.

The first meeting held in the completed house was in 11th month 1986; at that time, electricity, heating, a hearth, septic system, and landscaping were all in place.

The project was originally funded by Mrs. St. John.

The adjacent daycare center was given to the meeting in 1991 as a protection to both properties. It is used by the First Day school, but is managed by an independent board.

SOURCE: Materials furnished by Constance St. John, Bath, Maine.

South Starksboro Friends Meetinghouse

Starksboro, Vermont
Erected: 1826
Location: 7 Dan Sargent Road, off Route 7
Burial Ground: South of meetinghouse
In Use as Quaker Meetinghouse

South Starksboro Friends Meetinghouse, built in 1826 next to a "burying ground," is the oldest in Vermont still used as a place of worship maintained by Friends. The meeting itself has its roots in Creek Meeting for Worship, allowed in the early 1800s for "Friends living on Creek Road and adjacent thereto." By 1825 it was preparative under Starksboro Monthly Meeting, located at the north end of town.

In 1850 Starksboro Monthly Meeting was laid

down and Creek Meeting came under the care of Ferrisburgh Meeting; its name became South Starksboro Meeting in 1881.

Levinus K. Painter was very active a s resident pastor in 1921-23, followed by many years when a few families, the Youngs, Orvises, and Birdsells in particular, kept it going.

Rejuvenation began in 1970, when Middlebury Meeting Friends gathered together local well-wishers and others with South Starksboro connections for summer services, workdays, and special events—all well publicized. In 1975 the meeting moved from New York Yearly Meeting to New England Yearly Meeting, as part of Northwest Quarter and in care of Middlebury Meeting.

The 1980s saw major deterioration of the meetinghouse and Friends raised funds to fix it. Under the clerkship of Christopher White, the building was moved thirty feet to a new foundation; two years later, a First Day school building was completed. In 1996 South Starksboro became a monthly meeting and it continues to thrive today.

Source: Elise Barash, North Ferrisburgh, and Elizabeth Moger.

Vermont Meetinghouses No Longer Standing

Danby, Vermont

A large number of the first settlers in Danby, Vermont, were Quakers. The first meetings were held in a log house on a hill west of the residence (built in 1869) of Howell Dillingham. A regular meetinghouse was erected in 1785 on the southeast corner of a farm belonging to James E. Nichols. This meetinghouse, which also had a cemetery, was sold in 1806 to Ruben White, who used it as a barn.

A new meetinghouse built on the Dillingham property in 1805 had a burying ground. This meeting lasted until 1867, when the building was sold and torn down because the meeting had failed.

Because of the Orthodox-Hicksite split in 1827, a few members left to build an Orthodox meetinghouse in 1830 near the residence of William Herrick. Being few in number, the Orthodox Friends did not continue meeting, and the structure was torn down about 1850.

In 1845 a second meetinghouse was built on the east side of town where monthly meetings were held in rotation with the earlier meeting and Granville, New York.

SOURCE: *History of Danby* by J. C. Williams, 1869, and notes of Reverend Hugh Holland at the 100th anniversary of the Danby Congregational Church held in 1939. (From materials sent by Joan D. Bromley, town librarian).

Ferrisburgh, Vermont

The first Ferrisburgh meetinghouse was a large, two-story building that was shingled and unpainted. There was a gallery around the inside, reached by a narrow set of stairs. The meeting room had the typical two sides—one for men and one for women—that could be separated for business meeting by partitions. The benches were very plain and were faced by three long elevated seats, one rising above the other. In each side, there was a huge box stove. The meetinghouse and adjacent cemetery were surrounded by a fence. Two times a year visiting Friends were put up in nearby homes for quarterly meeting.

Following the "separation," the meeting remained Hicksite, but gradually declined; the building was eventually torn down. All that remains of the site are the former stone steps.

A second meetinghouse is presently a store. It was moved forty or more years ago from old Route 7 to its present location on top of the hill in Ferrisburg.

SOURCE: *Recollections of a Quaker Boy* by Roland E. Robinson and Charlotte Tatro.

Grand Isle, Vermont

This meeting was established in 1795; the first meetinghouse was a log cabin near the home of Mosher Hoag. Meetings were held there until 1827. A new meetinghouse was completed in the fall of 1827, about one mile east of the first building, near the Friends cemetery. This meeting continued until about 1860.

In 1899, descendants of former members had a boulder from the shore of Lake Champlain hauled to the site by oxen. It was inscribed, "Dedicated in 1899 in memory of the Society of Friends. In 1827, they erected a Meetinghouse near this spot where they worshipped for fifty years...and having finished their labors, they here lie buried and their works follow them."

"Quaker Monument" at Lincoln, Vermont

Lincoln, Vermont

Lincoln town history notes that many of the first settlers, who had names like Purington, Gove, and Guindon, were Quakers from Weare, New Hampshire. A preparative meeting was organized in 1801 and a two-story twenty-four by thirty-six-foot meetinghouse was built in 1814. This was the only formal house of worship in town until 1862. The meetinghouse was torn down in 1901, and the lumber from it was used to build a dwelling at 73 Taylor Avenue in Bristol, Vermont. The builder was George W. Farr, who was also an architect. The design is Italianate.

The meetinghouse stood on Quaker Road about a mile out of town past the town office. It was located at the site of the Friends burying ground now under the care of the town. On the way to it, on the right side of the road in a small fenced area, there is a large round stone mounted on a block. Dedicated to the memory of Chase Purington, the first Quaker settler, it is known as "the Quaker monument."

SOURCE: *Lincoln History Book*, published by the Lincoln Historical Society. Sandra Rhodes, town clerk. Adaire M. McKean of the Bristol Historical Society.

"Quaker Meetinghouse" - painting by Rachel Robinson.
Photo courtesy Stanley Farnham.
Was Montpelier Friends Meetinghouse.

Montpelier, Vermont

Meetings were held in Montpelier homes as early as 1795. A plot of land for a burying ground and building was obtained in 1809 on the present Cherry Tree Hill Road. A house that had been used as a store was moved onto the land in front of the cemetery by Johnson Gove, Ethan Hathaway, and Jared Bassett, Jr. In 2nd month, 1810, the amount of $115.74 was paid to Jared Bassett, Jr., for repairs. Timothy Davis was paid ninety cents for writing tables (probably desks for men and women clerks) that were installed at each end of the house. One of these is now believed to be at the Vermont Historical Society. There were partitions through the center of the building. Meetings were held Thursday afternoons and Sunday mornings.

By the mid-1800s attendance dwindled because of the Orthodox-Hicksite split in the Society and the strict regulation of members concerning simplicity, dress, speech, and outside marriage. The Montpelier Meeting was Orthodox.

After preparative meeting status was lost in 1832, Montpelier became an allowed meeting under the care of Ferrisburgh, Vermont Monthly Meeting. The meetinghouse was torn down in 1904, but New York Yearly Meeting still owns the site and cemetery.

SOURCE: *Across the Onion — a History of East Montpelier, Vermont, 1781 TO 1981* by Ellen Hill and Marilyn Blackwell, published by the East Montpelier Historical Society, 1983. (supplied by Marilyn Blackwell, East Montpelier librarian).

Mount Holly, Vermont

In 7th month 1803, Danby Monthly Meeting allowed Obadiah Brown to establish a meeting in his home. About 1805, Steven and Peter Baker of Danby built a small wooden structure just north of the road to Mechanicsville, Vermont. One report says this was moved into the village to become a home and may presently be part of a brick dwelling. The meeting declined and Samuel Cook and Aaron Rogers, appointed by the Danby Monthly Meeting, sold the property to one Daniel Peck for $35.

There was a Friends cemetery established in the southern part of the village on land deeded from Snow Randall on 8th month, 27th, 1813, to a committee of Friends. In 6th month 1849, Samuel Cook, the sole surviving Friend, leased it to Austin Morgan with the right for Quakers to be buried there "for as long as wood grows and water runs." On 12th month, 4th, 1857, the cemetery was conveyed to the Mechanicsville Cemetery Association for the sum of $50.

SOURCE: *History of Rutland County, Vermont*, published by the Mechanicsville Cemetery Association. Hughes and Bradley, "Early Quaker Meetings in Vermont," *Vermont History*, July 1961. Susan Corvella, town clerk.

Weybridge Friends Meetinghouse. This Quaker meetinghouse stood beside the Quaker cemetery. Note the horse sheds and the two doors—one for women and one for men, as was the Quaker custom.

Weybridge, Vermont

According to my informants, Weybridge was once known as Quaker Village. Quakers settled there about 1780 at the Lower Falls, where Samuel Meeker, a Friend, built a woolen mill. All that is left is a small Quaker cemetery near the river with most of the stones under the soil.

The first meetinghouse is said to have been built on what is now Field Day Road near the border of the town of New Haven, Vermont. After it burned, a second meetinghouse was built in the village. It also burned, and in 1835 Methodists built a church on the old foundation. This church was torn down some time ago.

There is a small Quaker cemetery in the village, which is maintained by a private individual.

SOURCE: President of the Weybridge Library Association, and Mrs. Wealtha Baker Bardosy.

Quaker Burial Grounds in Vermont

Creek, Vermont—
See South Lincoln, Vermont.

Danby, Vermont—
1) Southeast corner of farm which belonged to James E. Nichols in the late 1700s;
2) On property belonging to Howell Dillingham in early 1800s.

Ferrisburgh, Vermont—
The Ferrisburgh Friends burying ground is in North Ferrisburgh, going north on Route 7. Bear left at the Dakin Farm sales outlet on Old Route 7, also called Quaker Street, and continue a short distance. The cemetery is on the right, surrounded by an iron fence. There is a marker near the front identifying it as a Friends burying ground. It is very well maintained and there are some recent graves, but only a few markers are Quaker stones.

Grand Isle, Vermont—
Roughly a mile east of site of 1795 cabin meetinghouse.

Hartland, Vermont—
Quaker-Willard Cemetery, 1.2 miles north of Route 12 on Mace Road, north of the village of Four Corners.

Lincoln, Vermont—
The Lincoln Friends burying ground is located on Quaker Street about three miles past the town office. Shortly before it there is a clearing on the right hand side of the road where the so-called "Quaker monument"—a circular stone set on a base and dedicated to Chase Purington by his descendents—is located. Farther along, but well off the road on the right hand side, is the burying ground. It is on a knoll and is very difficult to see, but can be accessed by walking across a meadow and into an opening maintained by the town. Only a few of the stones are Quaker; the dates on them range from about 1815 to the recent past. Town history states that the meeting-house was adjacent to the cemetery, but there is no visible sign of a road.

Monkton Ridge, Vermont—
The Monkton Ridge Friends burying ground is a bit over two miles from the town center. Heading north, take the first left in town, then the second, and proceed through an apple orchard and past a four corners to a road on the right shown on the town map as a second four corners [now there is only the road to the right]. Turn right and go a short way; you will see a lane on the left that goes through a dooryard and down a grassed-over road, then through a gate. The cemetery is on a rise. As in the case of Lincoln, it has only a few Friends markers. It is moderately

maintained by the town, but there are some broken stones. There is a large tree in the center.

Montpelier, Vermont—

The East Montpelier Friends burying ground can be found by taking the first left past the village store when going east on Route 2. Go to the end of the road. At the corner of Quaker Road and Cherry Tree Hill Road, in a meadow to the right, is the cemetery. It has a gate and a wire fence. There is a tree in the middle, and the ground is overgrown with heavy grass. Many stones are down and broken. One source says that this burying ground is still under the care of and maintained by New York Yearly Meeting.

Mount Holly, Vermont—

Two miles north of town center.

Lincoln, Vermont—

Off of Quaker Street, about two miles north of town.

South Starksboro, Vermont—

On Dan Sargeant Road. Go south from Starksboro on Route 116, turn left on Route 17, take first left turn off of Route 17 (Purington); Dan Sargeant Road immediately to the right.

Weybridge, Vermont—

1) At Lower Falls, near river; most of stones under soil;

2) In section of town called Quaker Village; maintained privately. The Weybridge Friends burying ground is in a section of town called Quaker Village. Bear right in the center of Weybridge where the road is split by the town cemetery (you will see Route 123 to the left). At the end of the street in Quaker Village, where the road takes a sharp turn to go over a bridge, go straight into a private lane and past a large electric transformer into the backyard of a home owned by Mrs. Wealtha Baker Bardosy. To the rear of her property near the river, there is a mowed area surrounded by trees that contains only a few remaining and unreadable stones, the others having sunk out of sight. The site of a former meetinghouse can be found as follows: when you go over the bridge, turn right and go as far as the first corner, where there is an open field on the right. The meetinghouse once stood at this corner, but no foundation stones are visible.

Appendix A

New England Quaker Meetinghouses by General Architectural Style

Early Georgian-Federal—
[mostly two-story post and beam construction]

Adams, MA
Apponegansett, MA
Bolton, MA
East Sandwich, MA
Nantucket, MA (Pine Street)
New Bedford, MA
Newburyport, MA
Northbridge, MA
Saylesville, MA
2ⁿᵈ Seabrook, MA
Swansea, MA
Uxbridge, MA
Dover, NH
East Greenwich, RI
Little Compton, RI
Newport, RI
Portsmouth, RI
Saylesville, RI
Woonsocket, RI (1ˢᵗ)
Lincoln, VT
Weybridge, VT

Cape—
[mostly post and beam construction; several brick]

Casco, ME
Cobscook-Whiting, ME
Durham, ME
South China, ME
Vassalboro, ME
Hampton, NH
Henniker, NH
Unity, NH
Wolfeboro, NH
Jamestown, RI

Greek Revival—

Stamford-Greenwich, CN
Acushnet, MA
Allen's Neck, MA
Amesbury, MA
Lynn, MA
Mattapoisett, MA
North Dartmouth, MA
Smithfield, MA
Smith's Neck, MA
South Yarmouth, MA
West Falmouth, MA
West Newbury, MA
Westport, MA

Greek Revival (continued)—

Brooks, ME
East Parsonfield, ME
Leeds, ME
Limington, ME
Litchfield, ME
North Berwick, ME
North Fairfield, ME
Portland, ME (2nd)
Sidney, ME
St. Albans, ME
Unity, ME
Windham, ME
Center Sandwich, NH
Gilmanton, NH
Gonic, NH
Lee, NH
Meaderboro, NH
North Sandwich, NH
West Epping, NH
Westerly, RI
Woonsocket, RI (2nd)
Burlington, VT
Monkton Ridge, VT
Starksboro, VT

Late Gothic Revival—
[mostly frame; some masonry]

Lawrence, MA
Roxbury, MA
Worcester, MA (2nd)
Lewiston, ME
Oak Grove, ME
Portland, ME (3rd)
St. Albans, ME
Winthrop, ME
Manchester, NH
Charlotte, VT

Late General—

Hartford, CN
New Haven, CN
Storrs, CN
Wilton, CN
Cambridge, MA
Mount Toby, MA
Damariscotta, ME
Hanover, NH
Monadnock, NH
Providence, RI
Plainfield, VT
Putney, VT

Friends Meetings in New England, 1710

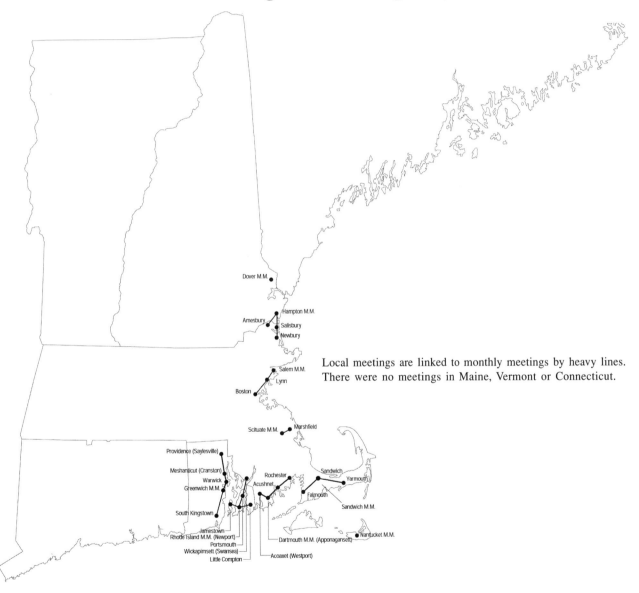

Local meetings are linked to monthly meetings by heavy lines. There were no meetings in Maine, Vermont or Connecticut.

Friends Meetings in New England, 1883

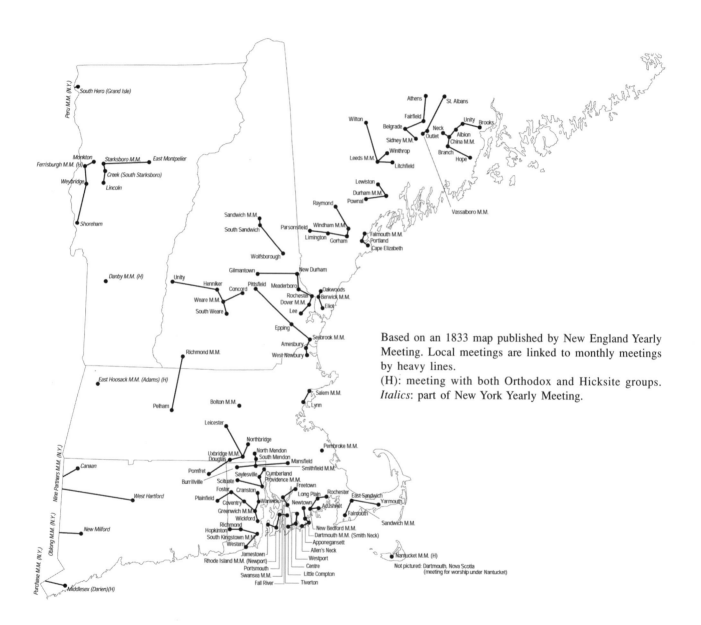

Based on an 1833 map published by New England Yearly Meeting. Local meetings are linked to monthly meetings by heavy lines.

(H): meeting with both Orthodox and Hicksite groups.
Italics: part of New York Yearly Meeting.

Friends Meetings in New England, 1997

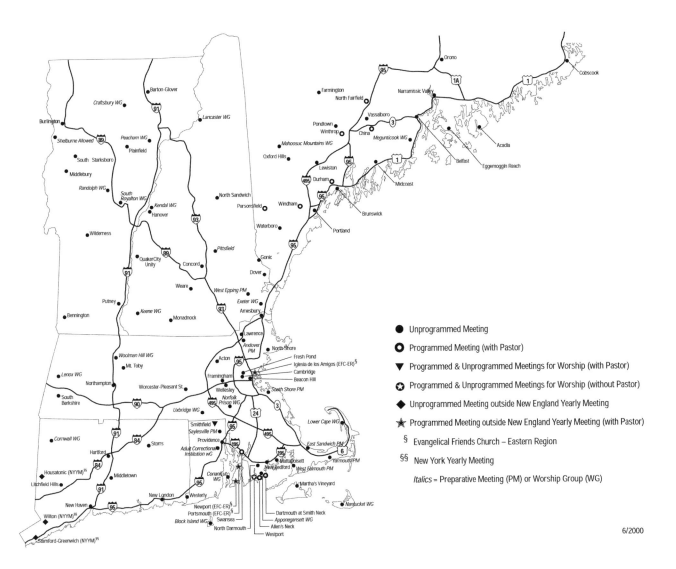

Unprogrammed Meeting

Programmed Meeting (with Pastor)

Programmed & Unprogrammed Meetings for Worship (with Pastor)

Programmed & Unprogrammed Meetings for Worship (without Pastor)

Unprogrammed Meeting outside New England Yearly Meeting

Programmed Meeting outside New England Yearly Meeting (with Pastor)

§ Evangelical Friends Church – Eastern Region

§§ New York Yearly Meeting

Italics = Preparative Meeting (PM) or Worship Group (WG)

6/2000

Glossary

Concern A specific task or issue a Friend feels led to take up; such a concern would be taken to a Clearness Committee to help the Friend discern whether they were genuinely led to undertake the work. SEE Leading.

Elder An experienced Friend who is recognized by their unprogrammed meeting as a leader; she or he does not have as formal a role as a programmed pastor but is generally respected and looked to for leadership in various ways.

Eldering The process of rebuking a Friend for inappropriate behavior; it is often, though not always, by an Elder of the Meeting. Quaker tradition and custom emphasizes the gentleness and forbearance yet directness with which eldering must be done.

Facing Bench In older unprogrammed meetinghouses, a bench or set of benches at the front of the meeting room, which faced the rest of the benches. The elders and ministers of the meeting would sit there during Meeting for Worship. These benches were often on a small platform.

First Day School The Quaker equivalent of Sunday School.

Fox, George The Founder of Quakerism (1624-1691); born in Leistershire, England, he lived through a time of much religious and spiritual turmoil and began the movement that quickly became Quakerism in the 1650s. He traveled to America in 1671 to 1673.

Great Separation The schism which took place in 1827-28 between the followers of Elias Hicks, a liberal Friend who emphasized following the Inner Light over the role of scripture, and Orthodox Friends with a more conservative, biblical bent. Philadelphia Friends split in 1827, Ohio and New York the next year. Differences between city and country Friends also played a role in the split.

Gurneyite Followers of Joseph John Gurney (1788-1847), an Evangelical Friend from England who greatly influenced mid-nineteenth century American Quakerism.

Hicksite Followers of Elias Hicks (1748-1830); SEE Great Separation

Laying Down (a meeting) The act of discontinuing a monthly meeting, usually because so few members are left that it makes more sense for them to attend another meeting. The term can also be used for discontinuing a committee or a concern.

Leading A sense that God is giving a Friend a specific task; Quaker journals often tell of Friends who struggled to discern whether a "leading" was truly of God and of the unease they felt until they acted on what they felt to be a true leading.

Minister Among programmed Friends, usually a pastor; among unprogrammed Friends, a Friend "recorded" or officially recognized as a minister who would often travel and work within the wider Quaker world to preach or pursue specific tasks.

Monthly Meeting   In America, a group of Friends and attenders who have Meeting for Worship together on First Day and have a Meeting for Business once a month. They usually, though not always, have their own meetinghouse. In other Protestant denominations a monthly meeting would be thought of as a parish or congregation; it is the basic unit of Quakerism. In England, this term refers more to what would be considered a Quarterly Meeting in America.

Orthodox   Friends who were opposed to the teachings of Elias Hicks and split from his followers in 1827-28. SEE Great Separation.

Preparative Meeting   A meeting which is preparing to become a monthly meeting and is "under the care of" a monthly meeting until it has enough members and experience to stand on its own.

Programmed Friends   Friends who worship with a planned service, usually with, hymns, readings, from scripture and a prepared "message" or sermon from a pastor. Some programmed meetings also contain periods of silent worship in which anyone may speak as led, as in the manner of unprogrammed Friends.

Quarter   Another term for Quarterly Meeting.

Quarterly Meeting   A group of monthly meetings, representatives of which meet every three months (i.e., "quarter") for business; also refers to such a Meeting for Business itself; quarterly meeting gatherings also usually include social time as well. Quarterly Meetings were more crucial when small, rural meetings were the rule. It is the grouping between monthly meeting and yearly meeting.

Unprogrammed Friends   Friends who worship in silence and do not have a pastor or a planned programmed service with readings, music and sermon; anyone may speak as led by the Spirit.

Weighty Friend   An experienced, usually older Friend recognized by the meeting for her or his wisdom, knowledge of Quaker ways, and spiritual maturity.

Wilburite   Followers of John Wilbur, the Rhode Island Friend who led opposition to the teachings of Joseph John Gurney in 1847, resisting Gurney's evangelical influence and emphasizing traditional Quaker values.

Yearly Meeting   A group of quarterly meetings, usually in the same geographical area, which meet together once a year at a weeklong conference. As with monthly and quarterly meetings, one both belongs to and may attend their yearly meeting. Nowadays many yearly meetings encompass workshops and social events as well as meetings for worship and business. New England Yearly Meeting (NEYM) is the yearly meeting for all but a few of the Friends meetings in all six New England states.

Bibliography

Barbour, Hugh and J. William Frost. *The Quakers* (Richmond, IN: Friends United Press), 1994.

Brinton, Howard. *Friends For Three Hundred Years* (Wallingford, PA: Pendle Hill Press), 1994.

Cooper, Wilmer. *A Living Faith* (Richmond, IN: Friends United Press), 1990.

Fox, George. *The Journal of George Fox* (Richmond, IN: Friends United Press), 1976.

Friends World Committee for Consultation, Section of the Americas. *1996 Friends Directory of Meetings, Churches and Worship Groups in the Section of the Americas and Resource Guide.* (Philadelphia: FWCC), 1996.

New England Yearly Meeting Faith and Practice, 1985.

Trueblood, Elton. *The People Called Quakers* (New York:Harper and Row), 1970.

West, Jessamyn, ed. *The Quaker Reader*, (New York: Viking), 1962.

Worral, Andrew J. Worrall. *Quakers in the Colonial Northeast.* (Hanover, N.H.: University Press of New England), 1980.

Editor's Note: The New England Yearly Meeting (NEYM) Archives are an excellent resource for further research on the history of Quaker meetings in New England. The Introduction to the Guide to the NEYM Archives is available online at www.neym.org. This introduction includes how to use the archives, information on Friends burial practices, and a list of locations for archive holdings. The Rhode Island Historical Society holds most of the NEYM archives. A hardbound edition of the complete *Guide to Records* is available for a fee. Write to New England Yearly Meeting Archives, c/o Rhode Island Historical Society, 121 Hope Street, Providence, RI 02906. Phone: 401-331-8575.

Index

About the Author

Silas B. Weeks

Silas Burling Weeks is a birthright member of Westbury (N.Y.) Friends Meeting, and is now a member of Dover (N.H.) Monthly Meeting. He is a graduate of George School and Cornell University, was a Kellogg Fellow at the North Carolina State Public Policy Institute, and attended the Rhode Island Graduate School in Community and Regional Planning. He is Associate Professor, Emeritus at the University of New Hampshire. In addition to his teaching career, Silas Weeks worked at county, state, and regional levels to address agricultural, community development, and public policy issues.

In 1956, Silas Weeks was among those Friends who worked to reopen the historic Dover (N.H.) Friends Meetinghouse, where he served as clerk of the meeting. He has been active on committees within New England Yearly Meeting and has served as a trustee of Lincoln School, Moses Brown School, and The Meeting School. He is a founding member of the New Hampshire Farm Museum and the Seacoast Growers Association. Silas Weeks travels among New England Friends with a concern for Quaker outreach and care for the environment.

"The ancient small farmstead in Eliot, Maine, which I have shared with Constance for the past twenty-seven years, has given me a deep connection, not only with ongoing natural processes but...with long years of country life down through the past," writes Silas. "English yoemen like the Odiornes, Goodwins, and Frosts cleared the land that we have cleared again. We have felled trees, drawn sap, raised and slaughtered pigs, chickens, and sheep, dried beans, shingled roofs, and plowed snow. (On it is) the private burying ground that includes farm cats Trouble and Underfoot and a new slate shoulder stone inscribed: Silas Burling Weeks, born 1st day 11th mo. 1914, died...."

JAMES A. TURRELL

Artist James Turrell began his career in California in the early 1960s as one of the leaders of a new group of artists working with light and space. His academic areas (he has a B.A. in perceptual psychology from Pomona College, Claremont, California, and an M.A. in Art from Claremont Graduate School) are reflected in his artworks, which make manifest the physical presence of light and heighten our visual perception. James Turrell's work has been exhibited in major museums around the world; several cities have commissioned permanent works. One of the second-generation Quaker's most recent works is a Skyspace in the new Live Oak Friends Meetinghouse in Houston, Texas. A member of Flagstaff (AZ) Monthly Meeting, James Turrell lives on Walking Cane Ranch in Flagstaff, where he ranches and oversees the completion of his most important work at the nearby Roden Crater (www.rodencrater.org).